OBAMA DRAMA

ISBN-13: 978-1548227692
ISBN-10: 1548227692

THE HOLLIS MEDIA GROUP, A DIVISION OF THE HOLLIS PROFESSIONAL GROUP

10 9 8 7 6 5 4 3 2

All images of Barack Obama and et al are Google images

Printed in the United States of America

CONTENT

ACKNOWLEDGMENTS

Neo-colonialism is essentially a strategy of deception. In the Obama case, capitalism (finance capital), and White ruling class power, gives the false impression of Black control, Black Power or real people power.

In reality, finance capital maintains control – politically and economically – and also controls the strings of a puppet leadership that gives a semblance and lip service to democratic concerns and populist interest, but in reality, it is the same old "oppression as usual!

DEDICATION

TO ELOHIN ISRAEL BY THE BLOOD OF YESHUA

- ❖ *My Parents: Willie and Anne Pope*
- ❖ *My Sister Barbara Bennett and her husband Carl*
- ❖ My Big brother, Willie Leon Pope and his
  Adoring wife Wilma Burgess Pope
- ❖ The mother of my children Ndanu [Dr. Pope]
- ❖ The Mother of My Children – warriors, Ndanu (Dr. Pope). She
  has been a friend through the years and a positive force for
  Africa and our children. I thank her for my children and
  helping to instill in them a commitment and dedication for the
  African Revolution. A family that makes revolution together
  stays together!
- ❖ My First Born – Akhnaton Natumbu Odinga Pope (The man of
  Destiny) and his Queen Eugenia C. Williams
- ❖ My Second Born - Azikiwe Tyeumba Odinga (Big Zike - Who
  stands like a Nation)
- ❖ My Last Born Menelike Sadike Ra Odinga - Sigidi Sikumbuzo
  Kumase.
- ❖ To my five grandchildren: Neffertiti, Akim, Amound, Kamau
  Azikiwe, Ndanu Eugenia
- ❖ Rasheeda Hastings: She has always been there for me, always
  encouraging and supportive
- ❖ Albert Seawright: A loyal friend and consistent supporter:
  Thank you brother.
- ❖ Bishop Melvin Brown. Thank You for your prayers, teaching
  and encouragement and all the ministers and deacons of Yeshua
  Temple of Praise
- ❖ To the core cadre of Sankofa community Empowerment Enc.
  Carry on the Youth make the revolution

❖ To Bishop Janice Hollis and Hollis Media; Thank you for being true to the spirit of "Freedom of Speech and Press." Without your courage to honor my constitutional right to freedom of press this book would not be possible. GOD Bless you Janice.

Foreword

Under the US Constitution, we have inalienable rights to voice concerns, oppose ideology, speak truth to power, and express our faith or lack thereof, and no matter how contrasting or stimulating, it is protected.

As a publisher [and a conservative], I knew this book would probably stir or ruffle a few feathers...needless to say, The Hollis Media Group took this project to provide an opportunity to an author who is protected under the same rights as all Americans regardless of one's faith, politics, socio-economic status or our belief in his truth.

Sometimes, we are forced to take another candid look in the mirror by what others view as their reality – more often than not, it is what we choose not to identify or address.

Introduction

This book started as a critical analysis of the Barack Obama presidential campaign. As soon as I heard that Obama was running for the office of the U.S. presidency, I began to do research on whom Obama was. My suspicions were that if the U.S. would allow an African [Black person], to even run for this "so-called highest office in the land," then the US had sinister and nefarious intent. My research proved right - beyond any doubt! I was particularly amazed at the finding of Barack Obama's membership in and active work and endorsement of the *Illuminati.* While most of the accusations against him concerning the Illuminati connections are proven completely unfounded when they're placed under scrutiny, although it can be easily seen that he does indeed have a part to play in bringing about the New World Order, the talk of which has only increased after he took office and the economy continued to plummet. Well known political figures such as Henry Kissinger and Gordon Brown have come out and openly endorsed the New World Order as a solution to the growing global economic crisis.

Many of the Obama Illuminati connections have to do with the powerful, elitist organizations which so many of his cabinet belong to; The Bilderberg group in particular, arouses suppositions as they meet secretly each year in order to plot out their plans for world domination. These meetings are by invitation only; the Bilderberger's organizing committee handpicks each attendee. The Obama administration practically reads as who's who when it comes to members not only of the Bilderberg Group, but other powerful international think tanks such as the Council on Foreign Relations, the Trilateral Commission and so on.

{See:http://www.rushlimbaughsites.com/opinion/the-barack-obama-illuminati-connection-754/#comments }

Deception was the order of the day as has been usual for US domestic and foreign policy!

In doing the initial research and writing, I had no doubt that many of my people (Africans and in particular Africans in America [Black people] would hurl acid criticism towards me for analytically attacking the "anointed one"! However, truth, like revolution, knows no sentimentality. I understood why many would think that the writing of," Obama Drama," was a betrayal to the cause and struggle of Africans in America; yet, I was also aware of the crisis of the colonized and oppressed. As Franz Fanon said in his classic book, <u>The Wretched of the Earth</u>, "The oppressed loved the ones they should hate and hate the ones they should love." On the other hand – a more truthful hand - I knew that only the truth would set us (African people) free and our people {Africans} and many other people, perished daily for lack of knowledge and critical analysis.

I do understand why many Africans in America voted for Obama; it was purely a reaction to the years of oppression and racism. It was an emotional reaction; it reflected the aspirations of millions of Black people. Many that voted had no prior knowledge of who Obama was not nor did they do any research on Obama's financial backers and *right-wing* political supporters. For many people of color, their vote was a hope that conditions would change. Africans in the US voted out of aspirations and emotions not serious research and analysis. This book offers a critical analysis.

Chapter One describes the basis and strategy of the Obama presidency, the financial backers of Obama and the intent of the US ruling class along with the thesis of the book that Obama is a strategy of deception. Chapter two outlines the domestic strategy of the US beginning in 2007. It has a recent update of the Obama administration and policy since he won the US presidency. It exposes the class nature of Obama and race-class struggle in the US, the Zionist connection and influence in the Obama campaign and presidency along with the callous views and domestic policies of racist US capitalism. Chapter Three parts A and B go into much detail of the US strategy for Africa and US foreign policy and the significance of Africa to world imperialism in terms of strategic location, its resources, and its scattered suffering masses around the world. Chapter Four offers a summary and a suggestion/ model for the future.

"And to him that has oppressed the poor and needy, hath spoiled by violence... he shall not live he has done all these abominations: he shall surely die; his blood shall be upon him." - Ezekiel 18

Chapter One

OBAMA DRAMA: STRATEGY OF DECEPTION – NEO-COLONIAL INTRIGUE

The African freedom fighter and philosopher, Junebug Jabbo Jones[1] would often say that "Mr. Say ain't nothing. Mr. Do is the man." While Barack Obama undoubtedly is the dream, pride, hope, and best candidate choice of millions of Africans in America and the hope or at least, the shrewd choice of many White Americans, as well as a significant sector of the US capitalist ruling class and racist right wing. There is much to be assumed that has not been said and much more to be revealed, that has not been adequately exposed concerning this "great White hope!

In spite of Obama's populist rhetoric, even with his advocacy for change and pledges of alleviating deteriorating social conditions facing average Americans and promises of tax cuts for working people, health care reform, better pay and a government that would protect pensions [not CEO bonuses], Obama's unquestionable political allegiance to his ideological and financial sponsors exposes his charade of populist rhetoric and confirms the suspicions of many Africans in the US – <u>at least those</u>

---

[1] African Folklore hero

16

<u>not in confusion and denial.</u>   Obama's undeniable political allegiance to his ideological and financial sponsors argues in a tenaciously and culturally embarrassing way for a person that has betrayed his people, prostituted his ethics, and as Franz Fanon points out in, "Pitfalls of National Consciousness"[2], shows Obama to be a willing instrument of his people's own oppression.

My parents would often warn me that the company you keep is a good description of not only who you are but also, what you are. The adage "birds of a feather flock together" has meaning with Obama and in this reference, he flies or is carried by political vultures and old eagles that now have very little places to roost or at least roost in safety. The dying buzzard of US imperialism needs a face lift, an image to fool the world, especially the African world. US imperialism needs to create an image of change, a deception needed to continue its *"Ugly American"* program of world plunder and greed. Those who choose to fly with the US will crash with it also!   Therefore, Barack can further insult the ebony polished legacy of Dr. King with speeches of "<u>our dream will not be deferred</u>", "<u>our future will not be denied</u>", and "<u>our time for change has come</u>." But, who is the "our" and what change is he referring to? Barack ain't with the masses and his change ain't what we are struggling for!

Obama's populist primary rhetoric is only one unsightly blemish of a face that stands before the flag of America and all the horror, oppression, exploitation, racism, and two-facedness that it represents. He stands for and promotes and pledges to uphold the law, even if it supports police officers who shoot tens of bullets into a Sean Bell. Even if the US law betrays thousands of Africans in New Orleans, even if the law ignores a tragedy like Jena Six. There is another hideous blemish on the face of Barack Obama and it is turned firmly towards the very corporate interests he publicly criticizes, which have poured tens of millions of dollars into

---

[2] Franz Fanon, <u>The Wretched of the Earth</u>

his campaign. It is a face – even if a Black face – that says I will be the mouth piece for a forked tongue foreign policy and a mask that will seek to trick many in Africa into accepting US strategy, US military, US intrigue, US capitalism and US neo-colonialism. How can you be for the little person while at the same time tenaciously be for the few that seek to live off the backs and misery of the mass of the people? As some would say in some communities, "we ain't falling for the dumb stuff!"

On the day after the Potomac primaries, *Business Week (the comic book of the ruling class)* ran a special report entitled, "Is Obama Good for Business?" The piece provided no direct answer to this question, but the attitude taken by the business magazine appeared to be a qualified "yes," based on the private discussions that the Illinois senator is holding with top Wall Street and corporate insiders even as he is delivering his public appeals for "change" and comparing himself to Dr. King. Remember it was Dr. King who got his head blown off for advocating a radical redistribution of economic wealth and power in the US. After learning of his victory in the Maine Democratic caucuses, Obama sat down at his computer to exchange emails with Robert Wolf, CEO of UBS America, one of his major Wall Street "bundlers," responsible for bringing in millions in donations from fellow multi-millionaires to finance what Obama refers to as his "movement." According to estimates made by the Center for Responsive Politics, <u>80 percent of the money raised by the Obama campaign that year came from donors affiliated with business, with Wall Street leading the pack.</u> More than half of the money came in the   form   of   donations   totaling $2,300   or   more.

In addition to Wolf, Obama stays in regular touch with Warren Buffett, the second-wealthiest individual in America, with a net worth of some $52 billion. Among his leading economic advisors is Austan Goolsbee, a University of Chicago professor and prominent advocate of free market policies; in other words, Obama is backed, encouraged, and financed by the worst of blood sucking capitalist. Yet, Obama out of his double-dealing and betraying mouth can say on the campaign trail such

18

hypocrisy as, he is concerned with helping "the father who goes to work before dawn and then lies awake at night wondering how he's going to pay the bills." Or "the woman who told me she works the night shift after a full day at college and still can't afford health care for a sister who's ill;" or the retiree "who lost his pension when the company he gave his life to went bankrupt;" and "the teacher who works at Dunkin Donuts after school just to make ends meet." Obama is full of the most toxic type of US capitalist garbage and vomits out of his mouth whatever his Zionist and capitalist bosses pour into his moral-less brain! As wrong as Hillary Clinton is, she was right on calling Obama elitist! Not only is he elitist. He is a dangerous subterfuge, a manikin polished by the best of media and Madison Avenue and most unfortunately for Africans in the US, a regime puppet that will dash the hopes and aspirations of millions. However, such is the hard medicine needed to jar millions of Africans in the US out of an addiction of denial and deception!

Obama: Class and Class Struggle

In Class Struggle in Africa, Kwame Nkrumah says:

"Class struggle is a fundamental theme of recorded history. In every non-socialist society, there are two main categories of class, the ruling class or classes, and the subject class or classes. The ruling class possesses the major instruments of economic production and distribution, and the means of establishing its political domination, {including the US presidency}[3] while the subject class serves the interests of the ruling class, and is politically, economically, and socially dominated by it. There is conflict between the ruling class and the exploited class. The development of productive forces influences the nature and cause of the conflict. That is, in any given class formation, whether it be feudalism, capitalism, or any

---

[3] Emphasis added by Odinga Mukhtar

19

other type of society, the institutions and ideas associated with it arise from the level of productive forces and the mode of production. The moment private ownership of the means of production appears, and capitalists start exploiting workers the capitalists become a bourgeois class, the exploited workers a working class. For in the final analysis, a class is nothing more than the sum total of individuals bound together by certain interests who as a class, they try to preserve and protect."[4]

Obama represents a sector or class of the Africans in the US that are hell bent on supporting the multinational class headed by the American ruling class, and Obama represents a sector or class benefiting from world imperialism and American capitalism; in fact, he represents the upper sectors of the African bourgeoisie. Be not confused by this term bourgeoisie! Especially for the African, it is neither best defined nor understood by just a simple analysis of income, type of car, wealth, neighborhood, and dress. Such items are not the best indicators of the self-centered and anti-mass views that this class holds as mandatory tenets of its elitist ideology. However, this is not to say that all who are a part of this class are dedicated to its values. As Amilcar Cabral very clearly states, some in the African bourgeoisie class have consciously decided to commit class suicide.[5]

---

[4] Kwame Nkrumah, Class Struggle in Africa

[5] Class suicide by the revolutionary petty-bourgeois leadership amounts to listening to its own revolutionary consciousness and the culture of revolution rather than acting on its immediate material interests as a social class. It must sacrifice its class position, privileges, and power through identification with the working masses. This unlikely event depends on the power and material basis of the revolutionary consciousness of sections of the petty bourgeoisie. The idea of class suicide by the revolutionary leadership is perhaps Cabral's most important message to socialist revolutionaries today. The absence of class suicide has blunted the progressive potential of many revolutions originally conducted under the banner of socialism.(See: Amilcar Cabral's theory of class suicide and revolutionary socialism Monthly Review, Nov, 1993 by Tom Meisenhelder. Authors's
20

Bourgeoisie in - a negative sense - is an ideology where those individuals who are considered members of the <u>elite</u> see themselves as a select group of people with outstanding personal abilities, intellect, <u>wealth</u>, specialized training, and experiences. Also in regards to the African - a group that sees itself as having favor by the ruling class of America who will reward good Americans ("good slaves") for their blind allegiance. This African bourgeoisie class views the masses of African people with disgust and seeks to avoid any contact with them; they look down their noses so to speak on the mass as ghetto, and will go out their way to make their disassociation and nauseating with the mass of their people such that it is clear to the White. They view the mass with contempt, and at every chance disassociate themselves with mass concerns and relations and will go so far as to make it clear to the White bourgeoisie class and even the White working class, that they are some miles apart, "in every way" from the masses of African people.

This is the kind of African that will promenade and boast that they are not Black - they are Americans. Some will even dare dress in African garb and attend ritual festivals, but their soul is in American capitalist values and their own reprobated greed and self-interest! They will support the cause of the US, even if it means turning a deft ear on the aspirations of the masses of Africans who – had it not been for the people's mass struggles - would not be in the positions of power and prestige that they currently occupy.[6]

---

note: Although I am not a Marxist, and neither was Cabral; this explanation is good for an understanding of Cabral's view of class suicide

[6] See; After Thought in Stokely Carmichael and Charles Hamilton's revised, Black Power: the Politics of Liberation

The following quotes by Kwame Nkrumah, from his Class Struggle in Africa, shows the significance of a class analysis for the African and reveals the uniqueness of this reality in terms of the African context.

"Each historical situation develops its own dynamics. The close links between class and race developed in Africa alongside capitalist exploitation. Slavery, the master-servant relationship, and cheap labor were basic to it. The classic example is South Africa, where Africans experienced a double exploitation -- both on the ground of color and of class. Similar conditions exist in the USA, the Caribbean, in Latin America, and in other parts of the world where the nature of the development of productive forces has resulted in a racist class structure..."

"While racist social structure is not inherent in the colonial situation, it is inseparable from capitalist economic development. For race is inextricably linked with class exploitation; in a racist-capitalist power structure, capitalist exploitation and race oppression are complementary..."

"In the modern world, the race struggle has become part of the class struggle..."[7]

Obama is the race card now being played on a neo-colonial level.[8] Obama represents a strategy that seeks to blur and hide the reality of class antagonisms (inside and outside of the African context). In addition, the racist policy of a capitalist ideology and stratagem, but this is consistent

---

[7] Kwame Nkrumah, Class Struggle in Africa

[8] The essence of neo-colonialism is that the State which is subject to it is, in theory, independent and has all the outward trappings of international sovereignty. In reality its economic system and thus its political policy is directed from outside. The methods and form of this direction can take various shapes. For a more definitive study see; Kwame Nkrumah, Neo-Colonialism, the Last Stage of Imperialism

22

with neo-colonialism which seeks to hide the real hand of power, a power that is quite content on manipulation from real sources of power behind the façade of a Black, media made smiling face!

Nkrumah warns and advises that:

"A determined attack must be made on the entrenched position of the minority reactionary elements amongst our own peoples. For the dramatic exposure in recent years of the nature and extent of the class struggle in Africa, through the succession of reactionary military coups and the outbreak of civil wars, particularly in West and Central Africa, has demonstrated the unity between the interests of neocolonialism and the indigenous bourgeoisie." [9]

American capitalism and world imperialism are in dire straights. American capitalism needs a new strategy to cope with the impending threat. A condition of permanent destabilization and drastic downturn is the order of the day for capitalism: the shrinkage of markets along with the scramble for sustainable resources. The political-military challenges, setbacks and defeats, the growing isolation of American ideology coupled with the world demand for debt payment. As well as the grave volatility of the US dollar, the internal growing resistance and growing misery of millions of hurting people, and the inevitable growth of a fascist police state, are a testimony that things are going very wrong and very bad in the good old USA. The American ruling class needs a 911 desperation strategy. But, like 911, the Obama Drama will be exposed, soon and very soon!

Deception, even mass deception, has been a stratagem of empires for centuries. Couple this old technique with the disabling abilities of a mass media with technological acumen, along with a colonized,

---

[9] Ibis; <u>Class Struggle in Africa</u>

disorganized and self-centered mass, and you have a condition of guaranteed control and exploitation. Obama is a tool intent on deception, media-creation, false promises, and contrived unconsciousness of the people. <u>Make the people think a change is coming, while you prepare for an offensive of domination and elimination.</u>

Although Obama makes sound bite references to the deteriorating conditions of working people - declining wages, rising medical costs, education and other living expenses, the shifting of jobs to low-wage countries - <u>this is not presented as the product of capitalism, and a social and economic system that benefits the wealthy at the expense of the working class</u>. Instead, Obama claimed, these conditions were the result of "lobbyists" in Washington who used their money and influence to crush good ideas and "politicians" who spend too much time trying to score political points instead of "trying to bridge their differences so we can get something done." In fact, Obama is only proposing to spend $6 billion a year on infrastructure repair – far less than the monthly cost of the war in Iraq - and an infinitesimal drop in the bucket compared to the $1.6 trillion the American Society of Engineers says is required to bring the nation's infrastructure up to good condition. Obama makes no mention of the 3.5 trillion that was pumped into the war arsenal for the US occupation and invasion of Iraq or the over one trillion for the US invasion of Afghanistan. Just the cost of one B-1 bomber ($200 million) could dramatically relieve the misery of a deteriorating domestic infrastructure, or improve the quality of education, food and housing in the poorest communities in the US. While Exxon makes 15,000 per second and brags of a third quarter net profit of over $9.92 billion, Obama speaks of a tax rebate of $1,000. With just the price of gas and bread, this will last only a few weeks and that is if one only buys bread and gas! While billions in the Katrina relief funds are missing, Obama, and those who dictate to him, are intentionally missing the need to provide for the "domestic tranquility." Obama is a strategy of deception and a tool of the ruling class!

24

OBAMA HAS THE ENDORSEMENT OF THE NEO-LIBERAL RIGHT WING

If politics makes strange bed fellows, then Obama has amassed a curious assembly of sleep around partners.

The Volcker endorsement

The endorsement of Obama by Paul Volcker, who was appointed Federal Reserve Board chair by Democratic President Jimmy Carter in 1979 and remained in charge of the US central bank - a Zionist instrument[10] - for nearly seven years under the right-wing Republican administration of Ronald Reagan. Volcker (another instrument of the American ruling class), was responsible for inaugurating a high-interest-rate regime demanded by the dominant sections of finance capital in the name of the battle against inflation. Volcker's monetary policy was inextricably linked to the offensive against the masses of many cultures and was launched with the firing of the air traffic controllers and the breaking of the PATCO strike and continued with the shutdown of large sections of basic industry and the unleashing of the worst economic downturn since the Great Depression of the 1930s. The venom of capitalism again struck without prejudice to all people notwithstanding, the fact that for people of color the poison was intentionally and systematically a huge racist overdose. The ultimate effect of these policies

---

[10] **ZIONISM**: this is a particularly sinister, racist and deceptive type of imperialism that hides under the concealment of capitalist governments, organizations and misguided religion. Openly it operates in the form of the racist-capitalist and morally illegitimate settler colony of Israel and an immense number of organizations. The Zionist movement is often times the hidden hand behind and within many capitalist powers and it is a major threat to African people and humanity.

was a vast transfer of wealth from the mass of working people to narrow financial elite, a process that has continued to this day. Obama applauded the Volker endorsement as a sign of people approval, but what people are we speaking of and how few?

In a statement announcing his backing for Obama, Volcker noted that he had previously avoided involvement in partisan politics. He said that he was moved to intervene now not "by the current turmoil in markets," but because of "the breadth and depth of challenges that face our nation at home and abroad." He added, "Those challenges demand a new leadership and a fresh approach." Obama's leadership, he concluded, would be able to "restore needed confidence in our vision, our strength and our purposes right around the world." I say." Obama is a strategy of deception!

Larry Kudlow, the right-wing pundit and former Reagan administration economic advisor, commented on the endorsement noting that he had once worked as a speechwriter for Volcker and describing him as a great American... a classic conservative... a man of fiscal and monetary rectitude. Volcker, Kudlow wrote, *would not have made this endorsement on a whim.*" Believe me. He never gets involved in these kinds of political decisions. He concluded by asking: Is Volcker the new Robert Rubin [the Wall Street insider who directed the Clinton administration's economic policy, a policy that was devastating to the poor, working class and the mass of Africans. Is it possible that Mr. Volcker is somehow tutoring Obama? Is it possible that Obama is more financially conservative than originally believed? YOU DAMN RIGHT HE IS!

These real relations are being forged behind the scenes as Obama delivers left phrases from the podium. Those like Volcker see the Illinois senator as a useful vehicle for effecting major changes aimed not at ameliorating the conditions of life for masses of working people, but

rather at securing the global interests of American finance capital."
Obama is a strategy of deception!

No doubt, the ruling class is gambling on that Obama, who would be America's first African-American president, is best suited to confront the dangers posed by continuing economic crisis and rising social tensions. Who better to persuade the masses not to rebel as they did in the turbulent sixties, who better to demand even greater sacrifices from the working class, all in the name of national unity and "change?" Who better to misinform and deceive Black people in Africa that that the "great White hope" of America; a savior and humanitarian solver of African problems.

At the same time, Obama would present a fresh face to the world, which the American ruling class hopes would help extricate US imperialism from the foreign policy debacles and growing global isolation that is the legacy of the Bush administration, and a failing neo-liberal policy. Given his big business ties, Obama's campaign rhetoric about confronting poverty and social inequality involves a level of cynicism and demagogy that is truly staggering. His incessant promises of change are not tied to any radical economic program that fundamentally challenges the profit interests of the giant corporations and Wall Street; and his media conspired comparisons to Dr. Martin Luther King, is culturally insulting and is as a-historical as Columbus discovering the western hemisphere!

On the contrary, and in ostentatious contradiction, Obama has advanced a neo-liberal fiscal policy, pledging himself to a "pay as you go" approach and stressing the need to reduce debt and deficits. I thought to myself, given the fact that he would take office with a near-record $400 billion deficit inherited from the Bush administration, and a plummeting US dollar, coupled by shrinking international markets and a peak oil reality, it is clear, or it should be clear, that the Obama domestic agenda - if he wins - will be one of extreme austerity measures, a growing and menacing police state, depression and a foreign policy locked into a strategy of attempted world plunder, desperation and increasing isolation, defeat and capitalist demise. Obama is a strategy of deception! I don't

27

think I was too far off then or now—this young president will continue to do damage on the domestic front.

On Wednesday, the candidate toured a General Motors plant in Janesville, Wisconsin and put forward a so-called jobs program involving investments in infrastructure and alternative energy that would total $210 billion over 10 years. In the face of the deep-going crisis confronting American capitalism, this is less than a drop in the bucket—and even this drop would quickly evaporate in the face of demands for deficit reduction. To the Military Industrial Complex, Obama has promised increases to a US military budget—which consumes an estimated $700 billion annually!

Those who don't want to talk about capitalism should by rights keep their mouths shut when it comes to poverty and unemployment. One cannot seriously deal with either poverty or unemployment without confronting the private ownership of society's productive forces and the immense social inequality that it has created. The defense of jobs and living standards, the right to decent housing, health care and education for hundreds of millions in America can be advanced only through a radical redistribution of wealth from the *super-rich* to the broad mass of working people. Clearly, the likes of Wolf, Buffett and Volcker are backing Obama because they know that he does not intend to go anywhere near such a policy.

It was millions in "startup money" from wealthy backers that made it possible for a very junior senator from Illinois, a man who four years prior to 2008 was serving in the Illinois state legislature and unknown nationally, to become a viable presidential candidate. The largely flattering treatment of the Obama campaign, by not only the liberal sections of the media but in the right-wing press as well reveals his class interest and support. Among those backing the Obama campaign are such pillars of the US political establishment as Zbigniew Brzezinski, national security adviser to President Jimmy Carter and co-author of the notorious national security Council memorandum #46[11] and arch-Cold Warrior; retired Air Force General Merrill A. McPeak. In addition, a host of other retired military brass; billionaire, along with Warren Buffett, the second-richest man in America; and an array of Wall Street and corporate executives, none of whom could be suspected of any sympathy for radical social change. This Robber Barron assemble of selfishness and callous mass contemptible profiteers of doom, have never and will never have any sympathy or regards for the rights of the masses of the people. It is to this host of evils that Obama and Mitchell pledge their allegiance to. *Oh! I know what you are saying. If not Obama then who or what? Keep reading! I'm saving the desert until last!*

Obama is merely the product of an effective marketing campaign which has utilized media savvy and technology to sell this new version of a very old product - the Democratic Party "friend of the people,"

---

[11] National Secret Security Council Memorandum 46, advanced by Nixon's National Security Advisor, Henry Kissinger, called for massive Third World depopulation among efforts to maintain the economic alignment of the superpowers. Zbigniew Brzezinski, who replaced Dr. Kissinger for the Carter administration, secretly dispatched National Security Memorandum 46 to cabinet chiefs only. This document, the most telling, authorized the FBI and CIA to initiate genocidal policies. Genocide is defined as the mass killing of people for economic, political, and/or ideological reasons. According to Dr. Horowitz, this term is contextually consistent with Dr. Kissinger's security policy that specifically cited the economic need to dramatically reduce the African populations, and Brzezinski's memorandum explained **that Black Nationalism posed both economic and security threats to America, according to Brzezinski, the most serious**

BECAUSE THOU HAS SPOILED MANY NATIONS, ALL THE REMNANT OF THE PEOPLE SHALL SPOIL THEE.
HABAKKUK 2

previously disgustingly incarnated in the "insurgent" candidacy of Jimmy Carter in 1976, then in the "man from Hope," Bill Clinton himself, in 1992. An Obama presidency would no more represent a fundamental change in American politics than the election of Carter and Clinton or the election of Lincoln, Roosevelt or Kennedy and if the Obama presidency-hopeful did, it would never be allowed anywhere near a presidential campaign!

Chapter Two

The Domestic Strategy

The initial writing of this book began when Barack Obama first announced his intent to run for the office of the US presidency in February 10, 2007. Most of the book was completed by the first few months of his presidency. The policies and events that have transpired since 2007 have confirmed much that was said in the initial writing. However, a few updates only serve to make more concerts the essence of this book and that is clear proof that the Obama presidency is a strategy of the US ruling class and an act of enormous deception. Barack Obama's first months have been dominated by a global economic crisis, a continuing war in Iraq and an escalation of US aggression in Afghanistan - continuing the militarist and aggressive thrust of the Bush administration's policies. A devastation of jobs, health care and public education of a scale not seen since the Great Depression, and intervention in court cases to lock away as state secret information about the massive government spying operation directed against the population.

Obama's first 100 days have made clear the right-wing character of his administration and the class interests it serves. This can be seen in just highlighting a few topics relative to the Obama administration in 2011: the attack on workers, health care, domestic welfare, and public education. As well as the invasion of Libya and Obama disdain for his own people – the African born in the US.

ATTACK ON WORKERS - The Job Crisis in America

In 2011, working people in the US are experiencing the worst mass unemployment since the depression years of the 1930s. States throughout America are making severe cuts in unemployment payments while bankers, CEOs and corporate profits are flourishing in downpours of wealth and luxuries. The Obama administration and the ruling hand that guides it lead the vindictive and punitive measures which threaten millions of workers and poor families with destitution.

President Obama dismissed concerns over the June 7, 2011 disastrous jobs report during a joint White House press conference with German Chancellor Angela Merkel that Tuesday. The president suggested the figures—which showed an increase in the national jobless rate rising from 9.0 to 9.1 percent in May and the average length of unemployment reaching a record high of nearly 40 weeks—were an anomaly. Actual unemployment figures for young people in the US is at "staggering Egypt-like levels: 30% for all young people, 45% for young Latinos, and as high as 66% for African {Black} youth!" In addition, the White House is engaged in ongoing talks with Republican leaders to gut long-standing entitlement programs like Medicare and Medicaid in order to pay for the Wall Street bailout and the extension of massive tax cuts to the rich.

The administration's indifference to the plight of tens of millions of unemployed and underemployed workers is provoking widespread anger against the president. In one *Washington Post*-ABC News poll released, 59 percent of respondents gave Obama a negative rating for his handling of the economy. Eighty-nine percent of Americans say the economy is in bad shape; 57 percent say the recovery has not started and

66 percent say the US was seriously on the wrong track. Overall, the president only had a 47 percent approval rating.

See WSW Obama ignores worsening jobs crisis by Jerry White 8 June 2011

These comments of callous indifference "come at the same time as government austerity measures, the closure of schools, cuts to Medicare and Medicaid, and the layoff of hundreds of thousands of government employees on both the state and federal levels." The ultimate aim is to create conditions in which millions of people have no access to even the most basic government assistance, to create such levels of economic desperation that workers will take any job, at any wage." (See; World Socialist Web, May 30th 2011," The Job crisis on America)

"Whatever the talk of an "economic recovery," the jobs situation is disastrous. Eighteen states and the District of Columbia had official jobless rates of 9 percent or more in April, while real unemployment is much higher. Currently, 24 million people in the United States either want to work but can't find it, or are working part-time involuntarily. This figure is larger than the populations of Chile or the Netherlands, and is twice the population of Cuba.

Some 5.8 million US workers have been out of work for over 27 weeks or more. Economists estimate that one million people lost all federal unemployment benefits last year after being unable to find work for 99 weeks. Nearly two million people total are among this group of "99ers." (See; World Socialist Web. May 30th 2011, The Job crisis on America). The US employment report of June 2011 documented the horrendous reality of worsening conditions for workers and the unemployed. It showed that far from a recovery the mass of people in America face a deepening crisis more destabilizing and destructive than the Great depression of the 1930s. See:www.adpemploymentreport.com/).

This situation is part of a global deceleration of destabilization of the world capitalist system. The slowdown in manufacturing growth is global, extending from the US to Europe to China.

In a gloomy editorial published Saturday, entitled "Dealing with the Evils of Stagflation," the *Financial Times* for June 2011, wrote:

"Although the recovery has been much shallower than in past recessions, it is tailing off. The response of the international capitalist elite has been to utilize the crisis to launch a counterrevolutionary offensive against the working class. " There are countless indices of growing social distress in the US—record levels of long-term unemployment, millions of home foreclosures, a 70 percent increase in Food Stamp rolls over the past three years, a jump of more than 20 percent in the number of people enrolled in Medicaid, the government health care program for the poor. But the response of the US political elite—from the Obama administration to state and local governments—is to slash Medicaid, Food Stamps, Medicare and every other social program for workers, poor people and the elderly."(See: US Job reports; World socialist Web June 6, 2011). This comes as corporate America, is presently sitting on a cash hoard of $2 trillion, acquired through record profits and soaring stock prices achieved by means of wage cutting and virtually free credit from the Federal Reserve Board. CEO pay is once again exploding, with corporate executives taking home millions a year and some hedge fund managers receiving billions.

HEALTH CARE

The Obama administration and congressional Republicans are conspiring to cut trillions of dollars in Medicare and Medicaid, the programs for the elderly and poor. One study estimates that a proposal from Republicans to cut Medicaid—which the Obama administration has refrained from publicly criticizing—would raise the number of people without coverage by 44 million over the next decade. Now under the Obama administration, this scorched earth policy is entering a new phase. The first step was taken last year under the guise of "health care reform," a drive to reduce corporate and government spending under the fraudulent slogan of "universal coverage." Now, there is little attempt to hide the fact that what the administration is seeking is a sharp reduction in access to health care and other social programs.

It looks like Barack Obama won't be the health care president either. Obama's health care plan is <u>so full of concessions to drug companies, so crammed with a constantly growing list of bailouts and exceptions</u> for insurance companies:

The president and his party have already <u>caved in</u> to the drug companies on reimporting Canadian drugs, on negotiating drug prices downward and on generics.

This explains why Big Pharma, the same people who ran the devastation series of anti-reform "Harry and Louise" ads to spike the Clinton-era drive to fix health care are <u>spending $100 million</u> to run Obama ads using the president's language about "bipartisan" solutions to health care reform

<u>Their plan doesn't cover the uninsured till at least 2013</u>.

2013 isn't "day one." It's not even after the midterm election. It's clear after the president's second term, if he gets one. Congress passed Medicare in 1965 and President Lyndon Johnson rolled out coverage for millions of seniors in eleven months, back in the days before they even had computers.

22,000 Americans now perish each year because they can't get or can't afford medical care, and this year three-quarter million personal bankruptcies will be triggered by the inability to pay medical bills. We have to question why this president and the supporting Democrats were in

35

such a hurry to pass health care early in his tenure that doesn't take effect until two elections down the road. It doesn't make sense in any kind of good way.

The president and his party have received more money from private insurers and the for-profit health care industry than even Republicans, with the president alone <u>taking $19 million in the 2008 election cycle alone,</u> more than all his Republican, Democratic and independent rivals combined

THE MESS OF DOMESTIC WELFARE of the 1%, by the 1%, for the 1%:

Since the Obama administration there are over 4 million more Americans living in poverty and poor people make up 15.7 percent of the population, according to new figures for 2009 released by the US Census Bureau. Taking into account living costs such as medical expenses, transportation and child care as well as non-cash benefits including Medicare, food stamps and low-income tax subsidies—the Census Bureau estimated there were 47.8 million people living in poverty in the US in 2009.(See: World socialist Web Site; Using new formula, Census Bureau ups estimate of US poverty rate to 15.7 percent.)

Among the sadistic statistic is an increase of poverty for the elderly. According to the official poverty figures, 8.9 percent of those 65 and older were living in poverty in 2009. But when out-of-pocket medical costs and other expenses are taken into account, the elderly poverty rate nearly doubles to 16.1 percent. The highest poverty rate is among children, 18 percent of whom are poor, according to the new Census figures

Both the traditional and the revised formulas vastly underestimate the real level of poverty in the US, since they both use an income threshold that is absurdly low. The official 2009 poverty threshold was an annual income of $14,570 for family of two and $22,050 for a family of four. The new Census figures were not even reported in Thursday's print editions of the New York Times, the Washington Post or the Wall Street Journal. This reflects the indifference of the political and media establishment to the acute and worsening social distress in the country and the vast chasm separating the ruling elite from the people.

The Obama administration is spearheading the attack on domestic welfare. This follows the extension of the Bush-era tax cuts for the rich, which will funnel some $70 billion a year into the coffers of the wealthiest 2 percent of the population, and the lowering of the estate tax, which will award some 6,600 families an estimated $23 billion in tax breaks. The Obama administration is intensifying the pro-corporate policies that have led to a massive growth of social inequality over the past three decades. The Economic Policy Institute (EPI) reported that the wealth of the richest 1 percent of US households in 2009 was 225 times greater than the median family net worth in America.

The record figure underscores how the ruling elite have used the financial crisis and recession to plunder social wealth. The ratio of the wealthiest 1 percent to median wealth last year was nearly twice the ratio of 125 in 1960.*(See: World socialist Web Site; Using new formula, Census Bureau ups estimate of US poverty rate to 15.7 percent.).*

Yet, as Columbia University professor, Joseph E. Stiglitz comments in Vanity Fair 1 percent of the people take nearly a quarter of the nation's income—an inequality even the wealthy will come to regret. "THE FAT AND THE FURIOUS The top 1 percent may have the best houses, educations, and lifestyles, says the author, but "their fate is bound up with how the other 99 percent live."

(See: Of the 1%, by the 1%, for the 1% in Vanity fair)

As the common worker and the poor cascade down the ugly but true side of the American nightmare, corporate profitability has rebounded, reaching the highest level ever, $1.68 trillion, in 2010, up 36.8 percent in a single year. Profits have increased 61.5 percent from the low point in the 2008 financial crisis that triggered the ongoing economic slump. With the help of the Obama administration stocks and profits for the super-rich has rebounded, with prices up 70 percent from the low point in 2008-2009, and a whopping $1 trillion added to stock values in 2010 alone. CEO pay is back to the stratospheric levels that prevailed before the crash, up 50 percent from 2009 to 2010, while pay levels for average workers have stagnated.

In fact, all of the administration's policies represent a continuation and deepening of the rightwing policies of the Bush administration. The Obama administration expanded the bailout of Wall Street begun under the Bush administration, devoting the full resources of the federal treasury to rescuing the banks and safeguarding the accumulated wealth of the financial elite.

Two-and-a-half year later, corporate profitability has been restored, reaching the highest level ever, $1.68 trillion in 2010, up 36.8 percent in a single year. Profits have increased 61.5 percent from the low point in the 2008 financial crisis that triggered the ongoing economic slump.

For the common person there has been no recovery. Instead, the Obama administration has spearheaded a drive by corporate America to make the working class pay for the financial crisis and bailout, through the destruction of seven million jobs, the slashing of pay and benefits, and an unprecedented attack on public services and social programs.

State and local governments have slashed 400,000 jobs over the past two years, and are now engaged in the biggest attacks on jobs, social benefits and workers' rights since the Great Depression. Wisconsin has provided the most publicized example, but Democratic governors as well as Republican are engaged in slashing wages and benefits for public employees, cutting or eliminating Medicaid benefits and other state services.

These state cuts will be dwarfed by the impact of the coming attack on federally funded social programs. The down payment will come in the cuts in current federal spending, some $30 to $60 billion, which the Obama administration and Congress are expected to finalize soon.

PUBLIC EDUCATION OR THE LACK OF IT

The American capitalist ruling class by way of the deceptive mouthing of the Obama administration proclaims that a major concern for the uplift of society and I might add the alternative to "reparations "for the African in America is by way of improving public education. Nevertheless, efforts of positive and progressive forces to improve public education in the US for over 150 years, is being dismantled. Cities throughout the country are closing public schools, expanding private charter schools, increasing class sizes, laying off thousands of teachers, and imposing sharp cuts in pay and benefits. In response to cuts in state funding, public colleges and universities are raising tuition to levels unaffordable to the vast majority of working class families with teens who are college age. State governments have passed legislation targeting the basic right to **resist** collectively the demands of the corporations and states. Several states, including most recently the Democratic-controlled government in Massachusetts, have followed the lead of Wisconsin in passing laws that rip up existing contracts with state employees and prohibit strikes.

This attack on public education takes place at the same time as the sums of money controlled by the wealthy reach record highs. Corporate profits in the first quarter of this year will break the record set the previous quarter of $1.68 trillion at an annualized rate. CEO pay for 2010 exceeded the previous record levels set prior to the crash. The combined net wealth of just the 400 richest Americans is, at last count, $1.37 trillion—approximately the same amount that would be saved over an entire decade through cuts in Medicaid that will threaten the lives and health of millions of people.

Obama has already been dubbed the "billion-dollar candidate," since his campaign is expected to be the first in US history to raise and spend that enormous sum. The number is appropriate and symbolic, given that the Obama presidency has served the billionaires at the expense of American working people.

High rollers will be called upon to do even more in the 2012 campaign. At a meeting last month, campaign manager Jim Messina asked 450 top "bundlers" to raise $350,000 apiece in 2011—the year before the election—double what they were asked to raise for the whole 2008 campaign. This effort alone would give Obama a war chest of more than $150 million going into January 2012, far more than any of his potential rivals in either big business party. In accumulating such vast sums of money so quickly, the administration is seeking to preclude any possibility of a challenge to the pro-corporate policies that both political parties uphold.

OBAMA and AFRICANS IN THE US {African *American* unemployment remains at over 15 percent}

The two interesting facts below bring to light the loathing that Barack Obama has for his own people.

1. **African American {Africans in America} unemployment remains at over 15 percent. as high as 66 percent for African{Black} youth**
2. **President Obama waded into the national race debate in an unlikely setting and with an unusual choice of words: telling**

daytime talk show hosts that African-Americans are "sort of a mongrel people." The president appeared on ABC's morning talk show "The View" Thursday, where he talked about the forced resignation of Agriculture Department official Shirley Sherrod, his experience with race and his roots.

Even one of system supporting conservatives such as Democratic Dr. Cornel West sees Obama as a tool of the ruling class. In an interview by Raw Replay last week, Dr. West suggested that Obama has sold out and become "a puppet" of powerful interests, merely promising change and not delivering. West warned that this would thrust the U.S. into a "democratic awakening" the likes of which the nation had not seen in decades.   Appearing on an MSNBC panel recently; West, remained outspoken. Amid a very heated discussion of whether President Obama is doing enough for Black people in America, he called the president "another black mascot" of "Wall Street oligarchs."

THE INVASION OF LIBYA: THE REAL REASON

On February 23, 2011 in a speech delivered with Secretary of State Clinton at his side, Obama announced that the government of the United States will soon intervene in Libya with its globalist partners under the threadbare cover of humanitarian aid and respect for human rights. True to his role as the first Black president of the US, Obama played his part as the mouth piece and voice of U.S. imperialism and hegemony, particularly as it relates to the new scramble for the riches , strategic location and resources of the most precious and expensive piece or real estate in the world, the continent of Africa. The U.S. has always hid its true intent of aggression behind a concealment of "democracy" – "demon-nacracy" and humanitarian concern. There is a historical precedent for such deceitfulness: the sinking of the battleship Maine in 1898 – leading to the Spanish-American war.

Controversy still surrounds the sinking of the Maine. During this period America was about the business of building its' imperial power. It sought the control of the Western hemisphere. Of course, such control trampled over the rights of the indigenous people, but America's aim was never justice but power. It was during this time that the iniquitous Monroe Doctrine was issued by President James Monroe. In essence, it stated that no European power could have dominance in the Western Hemisphere. In other words America was telling the world that we are the thieves of this area and no other thieves were welcomed.

The problem was that there was another thief, called Spain, which still had imperial interest in Cuba. America sought an excuse to fight Spain and chose to create the image that it was aiding the legitimate struggle of freedom fighters in Cuba who were fighting a war of national liberation against Spanish imperialism. The basis of this liberation movement was African and Latino. The battleship main was sent into the harbor of Havana where it was mysteriously exploded. Spain denied it. In Edward P. McMorrow's work, "What Destroyed the USS Maine-An Opinion", evidence is given implicating the hidden hand of America. America charged into war with Spain under the slogan, 'Remember the Maine.' Senator Thurston of Nebraska said war with Spain would increase the business and earnings of every American railroad, it would increase the output of every American factory, and it would stimulate every branch of industry and domestic commerce." Major-General of volunteers, in order to annex the pearl of the Antilles". In this contrived war over 600, 000 died.
The sinking of the Lusitania May 7, 1915 was a British-American plan to be co-conspirators in the deaths of its own citizens in order to create hysteria that would enable them to create a justification for America to enter the war. Although before 1915 America was trading with the "hated Nazi", after 1915, America saw it in their interest to come clearly on the side of Britain and France. After the war America would try to turn both France and England into American neo-colonies.

The Lusitania was a passenger ship. Years later it would be found that the Lusitania was carrying a large cache of arms that would be eventually used against Germany. By concealing them on the Lusitania, the allied forces could evade the very effective German blockade and submarine campaign. What is even more alarming is the fact that Churchill and Woodrow Wilson knew that it would be a very high probability that the ship would be in eminent danger, a fact that was concealed from the hundreds of passengers, many of whom were Americans. Ample evidence of this is given in Christopher's Hitchens book, Blood, Class, and Nostalgia. He shows that Churchill plays a strong part in the sinking of the ship and the controversy of blaming the Germans. Of course, America and England worked very close before and during the war. Both countries, by their silence and cunning, allowed the Lusitania to be in waters that would force Germany to sink the ship; however, Hitchens gives credible evidence that England - with American knowledge - sank the boat itself. This was used as one of the justification for America entering the war shortly after.

The Gulf of Tonkin Lie That Launched the Vietnam War 1964 "The official story was that North Vietnamese torpedo boats(PT) launched an "unprovoked attack" against a U.S. destroyer on "routine patrol" in the Tonkin Gulf on Aug. 2 and that North Vietnamese PT boats followed up with a "deliberate attack" on a pair of U.S. ships two days later. The **truth was very different. Rather than being on a routine patrol Aug. 2,** the U.S. destroyer Maddox was actually engaged in aggressive intelligence gathering maneuvers in sync with coordinated attacks on North Vietnam by the South Vietnamese navy and the Laotian air force. "The day before, two attacks on North Vietnam had taken place," writes scholar Daniel C. Hallin. Those assaults were "part of a campaign of increasing military pressure on the North that the United States had been pursuing since early 1964." On the night of Aug. 4, the Pentagon proclaimed that a second attack by North Vietnamese PT boats had occurred earlier that day in the

43

Tonkin Gulf -- a reporter cited by President Johnson as he went on national TV that evening to announce a momentous escalation in the war: air strikes against North Vietnam.

But Johnson ordered U.S. bombers to "retaliate" for a North Vietnamese torpedo attack that never happened! Prior to the U.S. air strikes, top officials in Washington had reason to doubt that any Aug. 4 attack by North Vietnam had occurred. Cables from the U.S. task force commander in the Tonkin Gulf, Captain John J. Herrick, referred to "freak weather effects," "almost total darkness" and an "overeager sonar man" who "was hearing his ship's own propeller beat." One of the Navy pilots flying overhead that night was squadron commander James Stockdale, who gained fame later as a POW and then Ross Perot's vice-presidential candidate. "I had the best seat in the house to watch that event," recalled Stockdale a few years ago, "and our destroyers were just shooting at phantom targets -- there were no PT boats there.... There was nothing there but black water and American firepower.

In 1965, Lyndon Johnson commented: "For all I know, our Navy was shooting at whales out there." But Johnson's deceitful speech of Aug. 4, 1964, won accolades from editorial writers. The president proclaimed the New York Times "went to the American people last night with the somber facts." The Los Angeles Times urged Americans to "face the fact that the Communists, by their attack on American vessels in international waters, have themselves escalated the hostilities." An exhaustive new book, The War Within: America's Battle over Vietnam begins with a dramatic account of the Tonkin Gulf incidents. In an interview, author Tom Wells told us that American media "described the air strikes that Johnson launched in response as merely `tit for tat' -- when in reality they reflected plans the administration had already drawn up for gradually increasing its overt military pressure against the North." Why such inaccurate news coverage? Wells points to the media's "almost exclusive reliance on U.S. government officials as sources of information" -- as well as "reluctance to question official pronouncements on 'national security issues.'" Daniel Hallin's classic book The "Uncensored War" observes that journalists had "a great deal of information available which contradicted the official account [of Tonkin Gulf events]; it simply wasn't used. The day before the first incident, Hanoi had protested the attacks on its territory by Laotian aircraft and South Vietnamese gunboats". Once again America had use lies to pave its way into war. One is not surprised that there are no weapons of mass destruction to be found in Iraq, although this was one of the main justification for America going to war, a war that will end in a victorious guerrilla struggle by the masses of Iraq. THE FACTS SPEAK FOR THEMSELVES!

Far from any humanitarian concerns or to the so-called justifiable rebels, the US –NATO invasion and bombing of Libya has all to do with Gold, oil, preventing a United Africa with a single currency based on gold, The fall of the US dollar, US fight for survival, The new scramble for Africa, and the Obama strategy and Africa.

First of all, only the most naive and poorest student of history would not know that NATO from its inception in 1949 was founded to counter the Soviet Union and its satellite states in **Eastern Europe**. The US-NATO coordinated relentless bombardment of Tripoli represents a new stage in one of the most naked acts of imperialist aggression since the wars of conquest launched by Hitler and Mussolini in the 1930s. Hundreds of people have been killed and thousands wounded. The bombings have demolished civilian government buildings, while damaging homes, hospitals and schools. Their intended collateral effect is to terrorize Tripoli's population of 1.7 million.

In an earlier period, such air attacks were described as "terror bombings." They were carried out by Hitler's Luftwaffe against defenseless populations—in Guernica during the Spanish Civil War in 1937, in Warsaw in 1939, in Rotterdam in 1940 and in Belgrade in 1941—

45

with the aim of annihilating the targeted country's armed forces, destroying its state and breaking the morale of all those opposed to foreign occupation. Acting under the pretense of enforcing a UN resolution and protecting civilian life, the US and its allies have caused immense suffering among Libyan civilians. They have likewise jettisoned the essential contents of the UN's founding charter, which outlawed wars of aggression and upheld the principle of national sovereignty, barring intervention in the domestic affairs of member states. Those responsible for these acts--Barrack Obama, David Cameron, Nicolas Sarkozy and others--are guilty of war crimes.

The Jamahiriya {People's Republic } of Libya in its current national and Pan-African perspective represents a serious threat to the Western imperialist and Zionist powers. The statement of Minister Louis Farrakhan in the last updated June 7, 2011, edition of the Final Call is quite informative as to the real motive of the US and NATO "If they kill Brother Gadhafi, I submit to you that American interests in Africa will come under severe strain,"…" "That man has invested in Africa more than any other leader in the recent history of Africa's coming into political independence," he continued. The Muslim leader said America needs access to the mineral resources in Africa to be a viable power in the 21st century. "How's America's wealth today? How is she doing financially? What is the deficit? Some say it's about $56 trillion counting Social Security and Medicare. That's a big number. She's printing money, but there's nothing backing it," said Min. Farrakhan.

In the book, *"The Fall of America,"* the Most Honorable Elijah Muhammad wrote, "One of the greatest powers of America washer dollar. The loss of such power will bring any nation to weakness, for this is the media of exchange between nations. Gadhafi's creation of the African Investment Bank in Sirte (Libya) and the African Monetary Fund to be based in Cameroon will supplant the IMF and undermine Western

46

economic hegemony in Africa," said Gerald Pereira, an executive board member of the former Tripoli-based World Mathaba. The moves are also bad for France because when the African Monetary Fund and the African Central Bank in Nigeria starts printing gold-backed currency, it would "ring the death knell" for the CFA franc through which Paris was able to maintain its neocolonial grip on 14 former African colonies for the last 50 years.

"The AU is the framework the Libyan leader was using to establish African self-determination and economic self-sufficiency. Col. Gadhafi financed the restructuring of the former Organization of African Unity— formed by African leaders Dr. Kwame Nkrumah of Ghana, Sekou Toure of Guinea, Gamal Abdel Nasser of Egypt and others—into the AU and revived the concept of a United States of Africa with one continental army and a single currency backed by gold."

Obama put forward a narrative of the events leading up to the Libyan intervention that was false from start to finish. "For more than four decades," he said, "the Libyan people have been ruled by a tyrant—Muammar Gaddafi." Last month, he continued, "Libyans took to the streets to claim their basic rights," but Gaddafi began "attacking his own people." While Obama decreed that Gaddafi had lost "the legitimacy to lead," the Libyan leader refused to listen, prompting Washington to go the UN Security Council to obtain a resolution authorizing "all necessary measures to protect the Libyan people."

Obama claimed that the US military action had been carried out "to stop the killing" and had successfully "stopped Gaddafi's deadly advance." In reality, Washington has intervened in a civil war that it played no small role in fomenting. The US Air Force along with smaller numbers of warplanes provided by Washington's NATO allies has functioned as the air force of the rebels, obliterating from the air troops loyal to the government in Tripoli, thereby clearing the way for the US-backed forces on the ground.

This is another deception. Placing military operations in Libya under formal NATO command no more removes the US from playing the decisive role than the formal command of NATO in Afghanistan makes the war there any less of a US operation.

NATO is dominated by the US military, which will continue to play the decisive role in the attack on Libya. Even as the Obama administration was talking about the winding down of US military operations, the *Washington Post* reported Monday that the Pentagon has deployed AC-130 and A-10 attack planes. These are aerial gunships that are used to massacre ground troops with heavy machine guns and cannons. As the *Post* noted, the deployment was an indication that the US military has "been drawn deeper into the chaotic fight in Libya." Moreover, the US ruling elite viewed with increasing alarm the signs that both Russia and China were establishing connections with Libya, in terms of oil deals, infrastructure projects and arms contracts, which threatened US interests in the Mediterranean and North Africa.

The aim of the military action is to install a more pliant regime—

 an out-and-out US puppet—in Tripoli. In the book I go into much more detail of the US Strategy for Africa and the role a " Black " president plays I this nefarious stratagem

"My own country is the greatest purveyor of violence" {from speech by Dr. Martin Luther King, "Why I oppose the War in Viet Nam.

Under the name of many US presidential administrations humanity has suffered. The US presidency and those who seek the oval office are only the face that people see.[12] *Obama is not the power but only the face that the power seeks to hide behind and so - as I have said before - this analysis is far beyond Obama*. It is an analysis that goes to the heart of the beast. It has been said that the greatest of the sins is not to show appreciation. The US capitalist system has committed many sins against humanity, and it has so very often hid its deeds of devastating devilish intent behind a smiling face. But smiling faces can tell lies!

Part two will focus on the domestic strategy of America's neo-liberal ruling class; a ruling class that is frantically trying to devise and implement the maintenance and expansion of a foreign and domestic strategy that it has been hell bent on since 1945.[13] This strategy has went under many names: "save the world from communism", "the Truman Doctrine", "Stop the Domino Theory in Viet Nam and South East Asia", "The New World Order", "Desert Storm", "the War on Terror," "Globalization" and we can be assured that the next administration - and the current ruling class that supports and backs the next administration - will also develop some "high sounding rhetoric" to hide its sewer low initiative of trying to oppress the peoples of the world. Whatever the name, the strategy must include a domestic and international line of attack.

The Obama campaign, in terms of its projected "media image" and aims, as well as the intent of the hand of deception that controls the puppet strings, has a definite intent regarding the domestic situation inside of the US, a situation that could turn ugly and radical given the inevitable contradictions that are developing domestically and internationally.

---

[12] **Who Rules America: by G. William Domhoff; Also see:** The Rich and the Super-Rich: A Study in the Power of Money Today: **by** Ferdinand Lundberg

[13] The Enemy; What Every American Should Know About American Imperialism by Felix Green; Also see: The US and Eurasia: End game for the industrial era? By Richard Heinberg New College of California (Santa Rosa)

The domestic strategy is a vital complement to both the international strategy and foreign policy of US imperialism; in both cases, it is a strategy based on a situation of desperation![14]

Externally and internally, the US ruling class must give the impression of change and reform while attempting to come to grips with the inevitable contradictions of a contracting empire and an empire that finds itself in the whirlwinds of competition and contestation from rivalry capitalist powers in western and eastern Europe as well as antagonism from the capitalist intentions of an awakening giant in Asia(China) - a giant that has a vested interest in building more and more with the tyrannical eastern "capitalist" bear Russia. One cannot adequately analyze or understand the Obama drama without having a correct analysis and understanding of US capitalism and imperialism.

"Modern capitalism has grown out of a horrid history and legacy of cultural disrespect, greed, racism, oppression, exploitation, conquest, invasion and a barbarism unmatched in the sordid history of tyranny and anti-people State sponsor terror.[15] While modern capitalism has used its accelerated technology to amazing heights, it has – on the negative side - corrupted itself and morally degraded itself to the slime of the most depraved toxic swamp.

The dialectic of US development is very unique. America is the most technologically advance society in the world today and at the same time the most politically backward society in the world today. America's insanity clearly is in the fact that it feeds on itself and will sell to itself the noose that will be used to hang itself.

Historically oppressive empires try to give the impression that they are invulnerable and that their power is uncontestable. Yet, history shows

---

[14] See: A Critical Analysis of American Capitalism In Crisis, by Odinga Mukhtar

[15] Ibid: Chickens Come Home to Roost:

clearly that empires come and go, rise and fall and are eventually brought down by their own evil endeavors, along with the triumphant struggles of those whom they have oppressed. Martin L. King would never tire of saying, *"The moral arm of the universe is long but it bends towards justice."* History also shows that when oppressive empires fall, they disintegrate astonishingly quickly! The American capitalist empire – and the myth of anointed Obama - will be no exception to this historical maxim. Not even technologically advanced and "sophisticate" America and not even media made Obama will be able to avoid the destiny with history. The conscious mind and trained eye, already has seen the genesis-doom and major tumbling of the pillars of American capitalism and imperialism. The political-economic crisis, which currently is strangling all capitalist nations, and the present crisis in the international situation foretells the requiem that will surely befall the American government and its economy of doom no matter who the smiling face in the oval office is. The "justice" forces of history will reclaim history, soon and very soon!" (See Chickens Come Home to Roost.)

The current international financial and political situation of world capitalism is characterized by a large quantity of destabilization, political-economic uncertainty, military expansion and at the same time military defeat and setbacks, a rising world condemnation and isolation, a growing anti-war movement within America and around the world, a decomposition of the anti-terror coalition organized by America, ground swelling distrust of the American ruling class, devastating setbacks in Afghanistan and Iraq, a mass "socialist-directed" upsurge in Latin America, intensified class and anti-neo-colonial struggle in Africa, a razor-sharp growth of mass revolutionary movements in Africa and throughout the Caribbean and Latin America, the growth of an American police state, an over stretched suicide prone US military, a critical rising unemployment - that is a crisis in the communities of color within America, a deteriorating heath situation among the American citizenry – particularly in the communities of color, a dilapidated housing market, a

51

government bail out of the housing mortgage industry that favors the super rich and condemns the middle and lower classes, an international banking and finance crisis, the beginnings of an anti-racist-anti-capitalist African and Latino youth movement in the US, an American military intervention which attacks popular governments around the world, neo-liberal and neo-fascist policies and an intensification of race-class struggle in the color *communities of the world.*

Things are not going well for American capitalism or any of the G-8 capitalist countries, in fact nothing has gone right or well for them for some time, and the current situation only increases the problems geometrically for the enemy of the peoples of the world. *"CHICKENS WILL COME HOME TO "ROOST"* The Obama drama is an attempt at distraction and tentative reform. It is an illusion and distraction as much as a super bowl, NBA series, movies, and crack cocaine; the illusion will only last for a very brief period and then reality, depression, frustration and rage will surely follow. .

At the very moment that American capitalism appears to be resilient, at the very moment that the oppressors gives the false impression of permanency and being at their zenith, at the height of the Obama drama, at the time that international finance capitalism manipulates its media and bourgeois scholars to portray a rose-colored picture of stability and growth, imperialism is entering its decisive period of decline, and empires fall quickly!

"For the day of the LORD is near upon the heathen: as thou hast done, it shall be done unto thee." -*Obadiah 1: 15*

As bourgeoisie economist and campaign tricksters match media hype with grand illusions of "things are really getting better," a new face is being applied to the Frankenstein monster of American capitalism in the

52

form of "Obama will bring about the change America needs", but the beast will not be hid for long. What better way to con-psych the people than a Black president? It is the old capitalist bait and switch game and unfortunately many are swallowing the con, hook, line, and sinker and Obama drama. But who is this new bait and what hole did this worm crawl out of? Moreover, how did they make this particular maggot so, butterfly attractive? "It's all in the packaging folks!"

The making and marketing of Barack Obama: Image and identity in US politics

With the exception of a popular sham showing in Chicago, the thinking and personality of Sen. Barack Obama, the presumptive Democratic Party candidate for president, was known by only an elite few just a few years ago.

Our brother Barack was born August 4, 1961 at the beginning of the turbulent and system shaking 1960's. Barack benefited from the mass struggle of the sixties which stood on the stalwart shoulders of the legacy of Black culture and resistance. His matriculation into Columbia University and Harvard Law School *(where he kept far away from mass struggle, mass issues and mass activism and interests)* was due not only to grade point average but mass resistance and mass bloodshed. As the *Times* notes, Obama, "whether out of professorial reserve or budding political caution," refused to take a stand on controversial issues. Also "he was unwilling to put his name to anything that could haunt him politically... 'He figured out, you lay low; moreover, while in school and continuing in his political career he kept distance from mass issues or direct theoretical or activist confrontation with racism and economic exploitation issues. It no surprise that he had little or nothing to say concerning Black people and the massacre of new Orleans, Jena Six, or Sean Bell. But those who struggle for freedom must be willing to stand up

53

for their rights! Laying low in racist Amerikkka will only get you buried further in disgrace and marginalized into shadows of obscurity;

The making and marketing of Barack Obama: Image and identity in U.S. politics. Had it not been for the blood and struggle of the masses of African people Barack would not have gotten near Ivy League academic status? Many in the African Bourgeoisie elite own their success to Black mass nationalistic resistance! Obama worked as a community organizer and practiced as a civil rights attorney before serving in the Illinois Senate from 1997 to 2004. He was a. graduate of Columbia University and Harvard Law School, where he served as president of the Harvard Law Review. He taught constitutional law at the University Of Chicago Law School from 1992 to 2004. Following an unsuccessful bid for a seat in the U.S. House of Representatives in 2000, he announced his campaign for the U.S. Senate in January 2003.

After a primary victory in March 2004, Obama delivered the keynote address at the Democratic National Convention in July 2004. He was elected to the Senate in November 2004 with 70 percent of the vote. As a member of the Democratic minority in the 109th Congress, he helped create legislation to control conventional weapons and to promote greater public accountability in the use of federal funds. He also made official trips to Eastern Europe, the Middle East, and Africa. During the 110th Congress, he helped create legislation regarding lobbying and electoral fraud, climate change, nuclear terrorism, and care for returned U.S. military personnel. After announcing his presidential campaign in February 2007, Obama emphasized withdrawing American troops from Iraq, energy independence, decreasing the influence of lobbyists, and promoting universal health care as top national priorities. *In Obama's legislative history there is no outstanding emphasis or advocacy for civil or human rights.*

Yes! He is to be applauded for his academic proficiency and marginal community activism, but his appreciation for the mass struggle - that forced open the Ivy League doors and system political legislative prospects - falls disgustingly far away from the contributions of such African legislatures as the Black reconstruction legislators or the moderate and radical legislators of the 1960 period that provide Obama with the opportunities that allowed him to be in position to announce his candidacy for the oval office of U.S. imperialism. The worse sin one can make is not to show appreciation! As David Walsh describes "Obama is the product of identity politics, which came to prominence in the 1970s. This opportunist trend, promoted by sections of the ruling elite, elevated race or gender above class position and served to undermine any organized struggle of working and poor people against their social oppression. It became a way for a relatively a small section of blacks, Latinos and women to advance themselves at the expense of the mass."[16]

Obama's right wing ideological persuasion and right-wing enthusiasm is seen by these comments:

Obama was largely shaped by the sharp rightward shift in American ruling class policy that began in the late 1970s under Jimmy Carter and fully flowered during the Reagan administration.

He was an impressionable 19, a college student in Los Angeles, at the time of Reagan's first election. In *The Audacity of Hope*, Obama offers this remarkable tribute: "All of which may explain why, as disturbed as I

---

[16] The making and marketing of Barack Obama: Image and identity in U.S. politics, by David Walsh
5 August 2008 (World Socialist Web.com)

might have been by Ronald Reagan's election in 1980... I understood his appeal... Reagan spoke to America's longing for order, our need to believe that we are not simply subject to blind, impersonal forces but that we can shape our individual and collective destinies, so long as we rediscover the traditional virtues of hard work, patriotism, personal responsibility, optimism, and faith."[17]

Obama says he opposes slavery reparations and apologies.
Fewer things in this world are more justifiable than the moral basis and humanistic sentiment and aspiration of reparations for the victims of the Atlantic - racist-capitalism – Slave trade, a crime against humanity. Even capitalist give forked tongue lip service to the demand for reparations; notwithstanding the fact that what one loses on the battle field can only be regained on the battlefield. The world-wide reparation movement by Africans is supported heavily by the masses of the people as the demands of the civil-rights movement were supported by the masses of the people; yet the "anointed one" is vehemently opposed to reparations. Tom-cat ain't going to do nothing that massa doesn't like! On this issue, the "anointed one" comes up like a sacrilegious garbage can maggot! Obama is a strategy of deception! (See: Obama Says He Opposes Slavery Reparations, Apology by CHRISTOPHER WILLS Associated Press August 2, 2008).

Obama says that 'government should instead combat the legacy of slavery by improving schools, health care and the economy for all. I have said in the past — and I'll repeat again — that the best reparations we can provide are good schools in the inner city and jobs for people who are unemployed," But this is not a position Obama adopted just for the presidential campaign. He voiced the same concerns about reparations during his successful run for the Senate in 2004. (See: *Obama Opposes Slavery Reparations - USATODAY*.com.)

---

[17] Ibid: The making and marketing of Barack Obama: Image and identity in U.S. politics

Some two dozen members of Congress are co-sponsors of legislation to create a commission that would study reparations — that is, payments and programs to make up for the damage done by slavery. The National Association for the Advancement of Colored People supports the legislation, too. Cities around the country, including Obama's home of Chicago, have endorsed the idea, and so has a major union, the American Federation of State, County and Municipal Employees. Obama has an embarrassing and consistent record of not acting, advocating or moving in the interest of the masses of Black people. Of course, this is a requirement to be a Tom-cat!

Obama – Tom cat and Tom Pawn in implementation of strategy to negate Black nationalism and ethnic cleansing relative to this discussion of a US domestic strategy and Obama Drama is the content and genocidal implications of an article by Glen Ford in response to an article in the New York Times, entitled, " Is Obama the End of Black Politics? Mr. When considering Ford comment the malicious strategy of US domestic colonialism is very apparent

"The Sunday magazine of the nation's most influential newspaper predicts that Black politics as we know it, is headed for extinction; that Barack Obama's "brand of 'race-neutrality' shows Black politics is obsolete, and should be abandoned." Of course, that's wishful thinking from a hostile quarter, based on assumptions that all Black politics is electoral. Blacks are becoming more conservative, and a generational crisis deeply divides Black America - none of which is true. However, Blacks have been set up for a fall. "To the extent that African-Americans expect more from Barack Obama than they got from Bill Clinton, they will be devastatingly disappointed."[18]

---

[18] **New York Times Attempts to Define and Dictate Black Politics: by BAR executive editor Glen Ford**

57

Barack Obama has a multiplicity of allegiances, <u>and the specific needs of Black People are not near the top of his list</u>. Again Mr. Ford comments:

"I would like to suggest that this country is already fascist and will only get more so in the future...for example look at the statistics about the incarceration of Africans...1 in 9 of every brother from 30-39 is in a U.S. jail or prison. In addition, 1 out of every 100 people in this country are imprisoned not to speak of the extra judicial killings lynching's, general racial profiling, the increase militarization and military aggression. For example, the sending of US war ships off of Lebanon to harass the Hezbollah and Syrian elements, lastly as Malcolm taught us so well, unity among our people does not mean acceptance of fifth column elements.

Conscious Africans have to have the courage to expose and oppose all those who are in the pockets or our enemies... Malcolm in fact told a story about how a young Chinese woman shot her father for being a traitor to the revolution there, and said that this is the way to deal with Toms...now we must all decide are we with Malcolm, are we with Kwame Ture, are we with Lumumba, Sekou Ture, Robert Sobukwe, Nkrumah or are we with the handpicked lackeys of white supremacy such as Obama, who is the creation of the Chicago Democratic Machine (the new version headed up by the son ... that is why Bill Daley, the brother of the current mayor is an important member of his campaign). Our people should ask themselves, why Obama has never done anything about the police killings of our people in Chicago. Why he has never said anything about the seizure of the property and destruction of the African communities in Chicago, and as I have been a resident of Chicago all of my life, indeed I lived and maintain a business office in the Hyde Park area that he represented in the State Senate, I know first-hand his treachery... I will say this, and this is the only thing I have positive to say about him, he did oppose the beginning of the war while he was in the state senate. However, that is more of a reflection of the general position in Illinois and particularly Chicago, as for example the Chicago City Council voted to end the war. Anyway, below you will find some info on McKinney's efforts with the *"Power to the People"* presidential campaign.

An Obama presidency (or a Clinton presidency, should her campaign ultimately prevail), would thus represent a fine-tuning or adjustment in American foreign policy, but no let-up in American imperialism's drive to war and conquest, which arises not out of the brains of George W. Bush and Richard Cheney, but out of the historical crisis of American and world capitalism.

Obama is merely the product of an effective marketing campaign which has utilized media outlets ranging from Rupert Murdoch to *The Nation* to sell this new version of a very old product—the Democratic Party "friend of the people," previously incarnated in the "insurgent" candidacy of Jimmy Carter in 1976, then in the "man from Hope," Bill Clinton himself, in 1992. An Obama presidency would no more represent a fundamental change in American politics than the election of Carter and Clinton did, and if Murdoch."[19]

Obama's Policy Solutions - or more accurately the policy solutions that the Obama campaign - have been given and advised to mouth by the

---

[19] **New York Times Attempts to Define and Dictate Black Politics by BAR executive editor Glen Ford**

US ruling class are contradictory and forked tongued demagoguery. Obama policy solutions point in opposite directions. Consider:

> *Rebuilding our roads and schools, taking care of our veterans and sending our children to college - How can this be done without drastically slashing the war budget? It can't. Obama is not thinking about cutting the war budget but increasing it and he is for expanding the war in Afghanistan, where – by the way – the US is experiencing a drastic defeat, as is the case in Iraq!*

> *How about providing jobs for all at a living wage? Can this be done without breaking with all the corporate "free trade" and privatization agreements? It can't. Obama walked out of the room during the U.S.-Peru FTA vote in Congress last summer -- so as not to upset his labor constituents -- but he praised the bill in the media, just as he praised "free trade" in his private meetings with Canadian political leaders prior to the Ohio primary. Obama, like Clinton, is a supporter of NAFTA, CAFTA and "free trade (free doom")*

> *How about providing healthcare for all? Can this be done without removing the private insurance companies from the healthcare equation?*

> *Obama says he is the man to stand up to injustice and he is the anointed one with courage to answer the red phone in some twilight hour but he allowed the racist US ruling class to "punk him out" to the point that he denounced his own pastor for telling the simple TRUTH. Obama responds and* jumps through hoops for the ones who really rule American capitalism.[20]

Obama the running pathetic dog of Zionism

20

Who Rules America: by G. William Domhoff; Also see: The Rich and the Super-Rich: A Study in the Power of Money Today: by Ferdinand Lundberg

Dr. Kwame Ture, correctly states that, "The litmus test of genuine revolutionary activity is anti-Zionism." Anti-Zionist or even pro-Zionism can be a barometer to assess, evaluate and even predict political behavior and moral viability of activist, organizations, movements, elected officials, ministers and religious leaders and presidents and presidential candidates - the two latter being historically "ball park ape enthusiastic" in support of morally filthy Zionism. Zionism, Zionist strategy and Israeli domestic and foreign policy decision and decisional results*{ operating with the policy of other governments and within the settler colony of Israel }* have not only been terroristically overwhelming, demoralizing and devastating to African people worldwide, but they have also been a scourge to humanity.[21] There is overwhelming and crushing evidence to the Zionist's military, political and financial backing of the worst crime against humanity and African people, the Atlantic Slave Trade. According to Dr. Leonard Jeffries, 75% of the financing of the Atlantic Slave Trade was supplied by morally bankrupt Zionism.[22] Any Black elected official that bows before zones (and *the majority of them do*) is puke treacherous and despicable to the depths of the lowest contempt! Obama goes beyond bowing; he prostrates himself before Zionism. When the Zionist tell him to jump his reply is how high boss and should I perform flips in the air and hit the ground running to lap up your vomit. The proof of such an acid criticism is in empirical fact! In a rough transcript that came from the Obama campaign of a closed meeting that the candidate held Sunday, Feb. 24, in Cleveland, Obama proudly stated:

---

[21] *Zionism in the Age* of the *Dictators,* by Lenni Brenner:

[22] Our Sacred Mission: *speech at the Empire State Black Arts and Cultural Festival in Albany, New York, July 20, 1991*, by Dr. Leonard Jeffries. Also see: The Secret Relationship Between Blacks and Jews, Volume I, published by the Nation of Islam

"I will also carry with me an unshakable commitment to the security of Israel and the friendship between the United States and Israel. The US Israel relationship is rooted in shared interests, shared values, and shared history and in deep friendship among our people. It is supported by a strong bipartisan consensus that I am proud to be a part of and I will work tirelessly as president to uphold and enhance the friendship between the two countries. The people of Israel showed their courage and commitment to democracy every day that they board a bus, kiss their children goodbye, or argue about politics in a local café. In addition, I know how much Israelis crave peace. I know that Prime Minister Olmert was elected with a mandate to pursue it."[23]

This is the same cat (Tom cat) that rejected repudiated and denounced reparations for his own people. "Puke treacherous" are words much too kind to label Obama! Tom cat goes even further to say:

"I pledge to make every effort to help Israel achieve that peace. I will strengthen Israel's security and strengthen Palestinian partners who support that vision and personally work for two states that can live side by side in peace and security with Israel's status as a Jewish state ensured so that Israelis and Palestinians can pursue their dreams. I also expect to work on behalf of peace with the full knowledge that Israel still has bitter enemies who are intent on its destruction. We see their intentions every time a suicide bomber strikes, we saw their intentions with the Katyusha rockets that Hezbollah rained down on Israel from Lebanon in 2006 and we see it today in the Kassams that Hamas fires into Israel every single

---

[23] Obama reaches out to Jewish leaders in Cleveland on Sunday, Feb. 24. By Ami Eden of the Jewish Telegraphic Association (JTA)

day from as close as Gaza or as far as Tehran. The Defense cooperation between the United States to Israel"[24]

It is clear whose interest Obama is primarily concerned with. But let us consider more The American ruling class and Obama's primary concern and support of Israel by looking at Zionism's and Israel's power and influence within American capitalism and world imperialism.

The power and influence of Zionism and Israel inside the US and within other world capitalist powers and puppet regimes is pretentious and formidable. Zionism is clearly a major form of imperialism, and has played a role in imperialism powers even before the infamous World Zionist congress meeting in Basil Switzerland in 1897 and it has played a major role ever since.[25]

Consider the facts from a research paper by James Petras; "The Power of Israel in the United States." Clarity Press, 2006.[26] J.J. Goldberg in his book, *Jewish Power Inside the Jewish Establishment* based on data in the early 1990's, noted that 45 percent of the fundraising for the Democratic Party and 25 percent of the funding for the Republicans came from Jewish-funded Political Action Committees (PACs). No single other lobby including Big Pharmacy, Big Oil and Agro-business plays such a dominant financial role in party funding.

---

[24] Ibid; <u>Obama reaches out to Jewish leaders in Cleveland</u>

[25] *Zionism in the Age* of the *Dictators,* by Lenni Brenner:

[26] <u>The Power of Israel in the United States</u>, by James Petras. Clarity Press, 2006

❖ **p14**

The basis of the [Jewish] Lobby's PAC power is rooted in the high proportion of Jewish families among the wealthiest families in the United States. According to Forbes, 25 to 30 percent of US multi-millionaires and billionaires are Jewish. If we add the contributions to the Lobby by Jewish-Canadian billionaires with assets worth over 30 percent of the Canadian Stock Market, we can realize the scope and depth of the Lobby's power to dictate Middle East policy to Congress and the Executive.

❖ **p15**

Who Finances the State of Israel?

The question of who is financing the Israeli state is basic because Israel as we know it today is not a viable state without massive external support. As the July 2004 updated Congressional Research Service Issue Brief for Congress titled "Israel: U.S. Foreign Assistance" points out in its opening statement: "Israelis not economically self-sufficient, and relies on foreign assistance and borrowing to maintain its economy." Despite what might seem an insurmountable obstacle not just to Israel's prosperity, but to its sustainability, the country has nonetheless done rather well. Billions of dollars are raised from a variety of Jewish and non-Jewish institutions to sustain the Israeli war machine, its policy of generous subsidies for Jews enticed to settle in colonies in the Occupied Territories and in Israel-sufficient to place the country as the world's 28th highest in living standards for Israel's Jewish citizens.

Without external aid Israel's economy would require severe cutbacks in living standards and working conditions, leading to the likely flight of most Israeli professionals, businessmen, and recent overseas immigrants. The Israeli military budget would be reduced and Israel would be obligated to reduce its military interventions in the Arab East and the Occupied Territories. Israel would cease being a renter state living on overseas subsidies and would be obligated to engage in productive activity-a return to farming, manufacture and services minus the exploitation of low paid Asian maids, imported Eastern European farm workers, and Palestinian construction laborers.

In the United States there are essentially four basic sources of financial, ideological and political support for the Israeli renter economy:

> Wealthy Jewish contributors and powerful disciplined fund-raising organizations.
> The US government-both Congress and the Presidency.
> The mass media, particularly the New York Times, Hollywood, and the major television networks.
> The trade union bosses and the heads of pension funds.

There is substantial overlap in these four institutional configurations. For example, Jewish supporters in the Israeli lobby work closely with Congressional leaders to secure long-term, large-scale US military and economic aid for Israel. Most of the mass media and a few trade unions are influenced by unconditional supporters of the Israeli war machine. Pro-Israel Jews are disproportionately represented in the financial, political, professional, academic, real estate, insurance and mass media sectors of the American economy. While Jews are a minority in each and every one of these categories, their disproportionate power and influence stems from the fact that they function collectively: they are organized, active, and concentrate on a single issue-US policy in the Middle East, and specifically in securing Washington's massive, unconditional, and continuing military, political and financial support for Israel. Operating from their strategic positions in the power structure, they are able to influence policy and censor any dissident commentators or views from circulating freely in the communications and political system.

Support for Israel from the US government:

The data below, compiled by the CRS [Congressional Research Service] Issue Brief in 2004, provide some notion of the extent of U.S. aid and special features.

* Israel has received more than $90 billion in US aid up to 2003, of which $75 billion has been in grants (i.e. nonrepayable), and $15 billion in loans.

* Since 1985, the United States has provided $3 billion in grants annually to Israel.

* Resettlement assistance for Soviet and Ethiopian immigrants peaked in 1992 at $80 million, but continues to be subsidized at $60 million for 2003, $50 million in 2004 and again in 2005.

* In 1990, Israel requested $10 billion in loan guarantees, which would enable Israel to borrow from US commercial establishments, with their loans guaranteed against default by the US government. In 2004, a further $9 billion in loan guarantees was included in FL. **1088-11.**

ONE CANNOT BE PRO ISRAEL AND PRO BLACK AT THE SAME TIME. ONE CANNOT BE DOUBLE MINDED AND WAVERING ON THIS ISSUE. ONE CANNOT SERVE GOD AND THE DEVIL AT THE SAME TIME: INDICATORS OF HYPOCRITICAL INSENSITIVITY!

GROWING CALAMITY

The following are more examples of non-compassion of US capitalism and reinforces the idea that one cannot be a good president of an evil political-economy. The dollar figures given show the abyss of disregard and the chasm of depravity of the US government and the executive office that would tolerate such immorality:

❖ **The money spent on war each day is enough to enroll an additional 58,000 children in head start each year, or make a** year's college affordable for 160,000 low income students through Pell grants:

* http://www.nytimes.com/2008/03/04/opinion/04herbert.html

* 13 Million US Children go Hungry each day! The Cost of one B-1 bomber $200 million. One in six Americans is fighting hunger. In 2008, 17 million households, 14.6 percent of households (approximately one in seven), were food insecure, the highest number ever recorded in the United States. Four million households became food insecure in 2008, the largest increase ever recorded (p. iii, USDA 2008). (To get population figures from family size figures, multiply family size numbers by 2.58, the average family size.) In 2008, 39.8 million people were in poverty, up from 37.3 million in 2007 -- the second consecutive annual increase in the number of people in poverty (Census Bureau 2010).{Also see: Hunger in America: 2011 United states Hunger and poverty facts; World hunger service. }

* For FY 2008, the Bush administration had requested $647.3 billion to cover the costs of national defense but just $5.2 billion a year: is the estimate for direct assistance to the most nutritionally deprived people on earth (Those starving to death- 214 million people. This has only grown worse with the Obama administration

* The US unjust war in Iraq and Afghanistan has cost "currently" $864 billion

* The cost of two B-1 Bombers (two hundred million) could end child hunger in the US! The cost of the Iraq and Afghanistan conflicts have grown to a staggering proportion of three trillion dollars

Poverty is the leading cause of hunger in America. Over 37 million people in the United States live below the poverty line and are at risk of hunger

---

- 12.5 percent of the nation's population lived in poverty in 2007.

  In 2007, the poverty rate for families was 9.8 percent, comprising 7.6 million families.

- The poverty rate in 2007 for American children under 18 was 18.0 percent, up from 17.4 percent in 2006.

In addition:

- 13 million children live in poverty in the U.S.
- The U.S. poverty rate for people 65 and over is 9.7 percent; 3.5 million elderly live in poverty.
- Of all family groups, poverty is highest among those headed by single women.

Study: Poverty dramatically affects children's brains by Greg Toppo, USA TODAY:

- A new study finds that certain brain functions of some low-income 9- and 10-year-olds pale in comparison with those of wealthy children and that the difference is almost equivalent to the damage from a stroke.

- "It is a similar pattern to what's seen in patients with strokes that have led to lesions in their prefrontal cortex," which controls higher-order thinking and problem solving, says lead researcher Mark Kishiyama, a cognitive psychologist at the University of California-Berkeley . "It suggests that in these kids, prefrontal function is reduced or disrupted in some way."
- As a whole, U.S. cities report that they are not able to meet the need for providing shelter for homelessness persons have a limited ability to meet the need for emergency food assistance.
- An estimated 24 to 27 million people in the U.S. turned to hunger relief agencies in 2006.

- 35.9% of American households receiving food from food banks, shelters and pantries have one or more adults employed.

The cost of direct US military operations - not even including long-term costs such as taking care of wounded veterans - already exceeds the cost of the 12-year war in Vietnam and is more than double the cost of the Korean War. In addition, even in the best-case scenario, these costs are projected to be almost ten times the cost of the first Gulf War, almost a third more than the cost of the Vietnam War,  and twice that of the First World War. The only war in our history which cost more was the Second World War, when 16.3 million U.S. troops fought in a campaign lasting four years, at a total cost (in 2007 dollars, after adjusting for inflation) of about $5 trillion (that's $5 million, or £2.5 million). With virtually the entire armed forces committed to fighting the Germans and Japanese, the cost per troop (in today's dollars) was less than $100,000 in 2007 dollars. By contrast, the Iraq war is costing upward of $400,000 per troop.

"In America, we need a radical redistribution of economic wealth and power"

Dr. Martin L. King

Chapter Three: The US Foreign Policy and Neo-Liberalism-
THE AFRICA STRATEGY {Part A}

"After reading the harrowing account of the brutalities of slavery, of subjugation, of deprivation and humiliation when whole civilizations were crushed in order to serve the imperialist interests of the West, when settled societies were disintegrated by force of imperialist arms so that the plantation owners of the "new World" could get their uprooted and therefore permanent labor force to build what was now the most advanced capitalist economy, it become absolutely clear that the only way out of our current impasse is through a revolutionary path- a complete break with the system which is responsible for all our past and present misery." A.M. BaBu from the Postscript of **How Europe Underdeveloped Africa** by Walter Rodney

"For evil doers shall be cut off: <u>But those who wait on the Lord</u>; He shall renew their strength.

"They shall inherit the earth."

(From the book of Psalms 37 and Isaiah 40)

Oh! If only those who made wars had to fight them; *and Oh! If US presidents and those who sought and seek that despotic office only had to pay for the wars they declared and the foreign policies they have endorsed and "mouthed to the people of America and the world,"* <u>then perhaps historic justice would roll down like a mighty stream!</u> But they will pay, as America must pay for the decades of deceit and the years of misery it has caused for millions! *(Image from Google cartoon images of Obama)*

In the name of the US presidency and under the misleading banner of democracy (demon -nocracy) , battleships and bombs, armies and arsenals, greed and malicious intentions have invaded the sanctities of cultures, and devastated the sovereignties of governments, all in the name of US imperialism! This fact alone would make any sane, honest and morally responsible person look on the office of the American presidency with derision, disgust and disassociation. Dr. Martin Luther King describe it with glowing moral insight when he said, "My own country is the greatest purveyor of violence in the world. **(See: "Why I oppose the war in Viet Nam:" by Dr. M.L. King Jr.)**

With totalitarian and racist disrespect and "a-moral' sadistic savagery, the history of US foreign policy and US relations with Africans and Africa has been and continues to be one of the most sadistic and unforgivable crimes against humanity! From the rape of slaves owned by old dishonest George Washington[27] , to the participation of the US - as an observer - at the infamous and divisive Berlin Conference of 1884-85[28], to the hundred years of lynching's during the reconstruction period after the American Civil War[29], to the Jim Crow legislation, segregation and institutionalized apartheid of the 1940's and 1960's[30], to the cruel castration of the anti-nationalist-integrationist-tokenism and COINTELPRO repression[31] of the nineteen-seventies and eighties and

---

[27] (At the age of eleven, he inherited ten slaves; by the time of his death there were 316 slaves at Mount Vernon, including 123 owned by Washington, 40 leased from a neighbor, and an additional 153 "dower slaves" which were controlled by Washington but were the property of his wife Martha's first husband's estate. As on other plantations during that era, his slaves worked from dawn until dusk unless injured or ill and they were whipped for running away or for other infractions. They were fed, clothed, and housed as inexpensively as possible, in conditions that were probably quite meager. Visitors recorded contradictory impressions of slave life at Mount Vernon: one visitor in 1798 wrote that Washington treated his slaves "with more severity" than his neighbors, while another around the same time stated that "Washington treated] his slaves far more humanely than did] his fellow citizens of Virginia. (See: Hirschfeld, Fritz (1997). *George Washington and Slavery*. University of Missouri Press, p. 11; also: Number of slaves: Henry Wiencek, *An Imperfect God: George Washington, His Slaves, and the Creation of America*, p. 46;

[28] 1884–1885 Berlin Conference, where only European powers sat and carved. up the African continent on a map—the United States sat in as an observer. See: How Oil Put Africa Back on the Map, by Ebere Onwudiwe
[29] 100 Years of Lynching's: Ralph Ginzburg; Also see: Black Reconstruction by W.E.B. Du Bois, and Without Sanctuary: Lynching Photography in America by James Allen

[30] CHAMBERS, BRADFORD; LINCOLN, DR. C. ERIC Chronicles of Black Protest; See: Black Power: The Politics of Liberation, Stokely Carmichael and Dr. Charles Hamilton

[31] See: www.cointel.org

right up to the current neo-liberal subterfuge and deception of the smiling face Obama drama strategy, the racist American capitalist system has been the arch enemy of African people and the masses of humanity!

Modern capitalism has grown out of a horrid history and legacy of cultural disrespect, greed, racism, oppression, exploitation, conquest, invasion and a barbarism unmatched in the sordid history of tyranny and anti-people State sponsor terror. While modern capitalism has accelerated technology to amazing heights, it has corrupted itself and morally degraded itself to the slime of the most depraved toxic swamp. America is the most technologically advance society in the world today and at the same time the most politically backward society in the world today. Its insanity clearly is in the fact that it feeds on itself and will sell to itself the noose that will be used to hang itself. Historically oppressive empires try to give the impression that they are invulnerable and that their power is uncontestable.

Yet, history shows clearly that empires come and go, rise and fall and are eventually brought down by their own evil endeavors, along with the triumphant struggles of those whom they have oppressed. Martin L. King would never tire of saying, "The moral arm of the universe is long but it bends towards justice." History also shows that when oppressive empires fall, they disintegrate astonishingly quickly! The American capitalist empire will be no exception to this historical maxim. Not even technologically advanced and "sophisticated" America will be able to avoid it's destiny with history. Those of us who are living in 2011 will witness the first major tumbling of the pillars of American capitalism and imperialism. The political-economic crisis, which currently is strangling all capitalist nations, and the present crisis in the international situation foretells the requiem that will surely befall the American government and its economy of doom. The "justice" forces of history will reclaim history, soon and very soon!

The current international financial and political situation of world capitalism is characterized by a large quantity of destabilization, political-economic uncertainty, nation-states on the verge of default, military expansion and at the same time military defeat and setbacks, disastrous credit devaluation by ,major western countries, a rising world condemnation and isolation of capitalist and Zionist State terror, a growing anti-war movement within America and around the world, a decomposition of the so-called "anti-terror coalition" organized by America, a ground swelling distrust of the American ruling class and the American government, an earth shaking nationalist rising within the Palestinian revolution, devastating setbacks in Afghanistan and Iraq, a razor-sharp growth of mass revolutionary movements in Africa and throughout the Caribbean and Latin America, the growth of an American police state, a critical rising unemployment rate in the U.S. approaching 10% nationally which is a crisis in the communities of color within America, a deteriorating heath situation among the American citizenry – particularly in the communities of color, the beginnings of a anti-racist, anti-capitalist African and Latino youth movement in the US, American military intervention around the world which attacks popular governments, neo-liberal and neo-fascist policies and an intensification of race-class struggle. Things are not going well for American capitalism, in fact nothing is going right or well for them, and this situation only increases geometrically for the enemy of the peoples of the world. "CHICKENS WILL COME HOME TO "ROOST." At the very moment that American capitalism appears to be resilient, at the very moment that the oppressors gives the false impression of permanency and being at their zenith, at the time that international finance capitalism manipulates its media and bourgeois scholars to portray a rose-colored picture of stability and growth, imperialism is entering its decisive period of decline, and empires fall quickly.

The global reach of the United States is backed by its' foreign policy by which the United States interacts with foreign nations. US

75

foreign policy from 1776 to present, in general - and specifically in relation to Africa - has been a policy and strategy of invasions, destabilizations, assassinations, State sponsored terror, deception, orchestrated coup d'état, (media, NGO and organizational manipulation) and a forked tong diplomacy, backed by a gun boat-air assault and infantry financed and backed by an over 13 trillion dollar economy and the new mouth of US imperialism, President Barak Obama, who is seeking to increase the military budget as he calls for billions more to bail out the super-rich!

The officially stated goals of the foreign policy of the United States, as mentioned in the Foreign Policy Agenda of the U.S. Department of State, are "to create a more secure, democratic, and prosperous world for the benefit of the American people and the international community."[32] **Nothing can be further from the truth![33]** In addition, the United States House Committee on Foreign Affairs states as some of its jurisdictional goals: "export controls, including nonproliferation of nuclear technology and nuclear hardware; measures to foster commercial intercourse with foreign nations and to safeguard American business abroad. If America – that is the American ruling class – interest is capitalist development and expansion – *AND IT SURELY IS* – then America is about the business of exploitation and domination.

The foreign policy of the US, in relation to the policies of the Obama administration or the administration of any occupier of the U.S. oval office, will only follow the path of the treacherous legacy that birthed America - a tale of genocidal assault on the indigenous of the Western hemisphere, the oppressive utilization of Asian labor, the exploitation of

---

[32] US Dept. of State - Foreign Policy Agenda

[33] The Enemy, What Every American Should Know About American Imperialism, By Felix Green

White workers, and the enslavement of the African. YOU CAN NOT BE A GOOD PRESIDENT OF AN EVIL EMPIRE!

AN OVERVIEW OF US FOREIGN POLICY

THE ATTACK ON PEOPLE'S SOVERIGNITY

Quite obviously, all US presidents since old dishonest George to "skinning-grinning" Obama have proudly endorse and attempted to rationalize and justify US foreign policy. But, an accurate and objective analysis of US history and international relations squarely places the US at the top of evil empires! The record speaks for itself:

"The bourgeoisie American revolution, the Spanish American war, the so-called Indian wars against the indigenous of the Western hemisphere – including the genocidal " Long March" in which over 16,000 Cherokee began the *Long march*, in which one quarter to half dyed along the way - the invasion of Africa by way of the Barbary Coast War, the war with British capitalism - called the War of 1812, the racist and expansionist Monroe Doctrine, the Roosevelt Corollary, the racist-fascist annexation of the Panama Canal, the expansion of the Rockefeller oil interest throughout Latin America, World War One and Two, the Korean War, the Truman Doctrine, the US marine invasion of Trinidad, the Bay of Pigs Invasion, the invasion of Grenada, the Viet Nam War, the wars with Iraq and Afghanistan, the proxy wars and US supplied and financed armies in Africa and Latin America, the numerous CIA sponsored assassinations, the overthrow of Allende in Chili, the overthrown of Nkrumah in Ghana, the overthrow and assassination of Patrice Lumumba in the Congo, the thirty five US backed successful assassinations that led to a regime changes- not counting the assassinations that did not lead to a regime change, the 737 US military bases around the world that aid the US in the control *of humanity's economic, social and political activities under the helm of US corporate and military power.* And the continued policy of imperialist expansion and war that is endorsed by Obama, all give repugnant testimony to the foreign policy record of the United Snakes! "[34]

"Fret not thyself of evil doers, neither thou be envious against the workers of Iniquity. For hey shall soon be cut down like the grass and wither away." Psalms 37:1-2

In his "A Brief History of U.S. Interventions: 1945 to the Present," William Blum, argues: "The engine of American foreign policy has been fueled not by a devotion to any kind of morality, but rather by the necessity to serve other imperatives, which can be summarized as follows:
 * making the world safe for American corporations *enhancing the financial statements of defense contractors at home who have contributed generously to members of congress* preventing the rise of any society that might serve as a successful example of an alternative to the capitalist mode* extending political and economic hegemony over as wide an area as possible, as befits a "great power.
* This in the name of fighting a supposed moral crusade against what cold war sees as the existence of an evil International Communist Conspiracy, which in fact never existed, ."[35]

---

[34] **Emphasis added by Odinga Mukhtar**

[35] A Brief History of U.S. Interventions: 1945 to the Present, William Blum

78

All the US wars and related foreign policy actions of the US have never served the interest of the masses of the people in the US, although the masses have died for what they confusingly thought was an effort to make the world safe and preserve democracy. But only the blind and unconscious do not see; for lack of vision the masses do die and suffer and will continue to do so if they do not gain consciousness. The ruling classes of US capitalism have no morally social concern for the people of America or the world! For the ruling class, the interest of the people is not even the last concern. With a deceptive smile on his face, Obama encourages the people to admit their faults, sacrifice and charge forward, while the conscious say, *"HELL NO! SAVE THE DRAMA FOR OBAMA'S MOMMA!"*

An Obama presidency would further legitimize and faultily justify the imperialist orientation and racist intent of US foreign policy by inscribing it as liberalism or the "new kind" of progressivism.

A CONTINUATION OF NEO-LIBERAL EMPIRE BUILDING UNDER THE DISGUISE OF: *Democracy {Demon- nacracy}*

"Neo-liberalism" is a set of economic policies that have become widespread during the last 25 years or so. Although the word is rarely heard in the United States, you can clearly see the effects of neo-liberalism here as the rich grow richer and the poor grow poorer."[36] For the understanding of this writing, a bit more can be added to the conscious description of Martinez and Garcia.

Neo-liberalism - similar to neo-colonialism - is an imperialist strategy to hold and/ or expand the immoral and empire predation, annexation, and seizure of people's land. It is empire building with a

---

[36] **What is "Neo-Liberalism"? A Brief Definition** by Elizabeth Martinez and Arnoldo García
Updated: February 26th, 2000 the-reaction.blogspot.com/2008/08/top-ten-clo...

79

deceptive title but imperial seizure nevertheless. According to Martinez and Garcia, the main points of neo-liberalism include:

1. *THE RULE OF THE MARKET*. Liberating "free" enterprise or private enterprise from any bonds imposed by the government (the state) no matter how much social damage this causes. Greater openness to international trade and investment, as in NAFTA. Reduce wages by de-unionizing workers and eliminating workers' rights that had been won over many years of struggle. No more price controls. All in all, total freedom of movement for capital, goods and services. To convince the public that this is good the intellectual apologist for neo-liberalism say, "an unregulated market is the best way to increase economic growth, which will ultimately benefit everyone." It's like Reagan's "supply-side" and "trickle-down" economics -- but somehow the wealth didn't trickle down very much.

2. *CUTTING PUBLIC EXPENDITURE FOR SOCIAL SERVICES* like education and health care. *REDUCING THE SAFETY-NET FOR THE POOR*, and even maintenance of roads, bridges, water supply -- again in the name of reducing government's role. Of course, they don't oppose government subsidies and tax benefits for business.

3. *DEREGULATION*. Reduce government regulation of everything that could diminish profits, including protecting the environment and safety on the job.

4. *PRIVATIZATION*. Sell state-owned enterprises, goods and services to private investors. This includes banks, key industries, railroads, toll highways, electricity, schools, hospitals, prisons and even fresh water. Although usually done in the name of greater efficiency, which is often needed, privatization has mainly had the effect of concentrating wealth even more in *a few hands and making the public pay even more for its needs.*

5. ***ELIMINATING THE CONCEPT OF "THE PUBLIC GOOD" or "COMMUNITY"*** and replacing it with "individual responsibility."

Pressuring the poorest people in a society to find solutions to their lack of health care, education and social security all by themselves -- then blaming them, if they fail, as "lazy."

The Obama administration marches to the toon of the neo-liberalist. In the United States, neo-liberalism is destroying welfare programs; attacking the rights of labor (including all immigrant workers); and cutting back social programs. The Republican "Contract" on America is pure neo-liberalism. Its supporters are working hard to deny protection to children, youth, women, the planet itself -- and trying to trick us into acceptance by saying this will "get government off my back." The beneficiaries of neo-liberalism are a minority of the world's people. For the vast majority, it brings even more suffering than before, suffering without end. The Obama presidency is a neo-liberal strategy of deception! To the untrained eye and the unconscious mind, it appears to be for the people. Obama media army, oratory skills, big smile and complexion adds to the deception but he is a ***colonial puppet!***

All forms of imperial territorial control and subjugation are {**essentially colonialism**}! Weather you call it neo-liberalism, neo-colonialism, cultural domination, etc., all imperial territorial control and subjugation seeks to dominate and ideologically penetrate the minds, cultures, institutions and lands of a people. In addition, all oppression leads to the underdevelopment and demise of the subject people.

Essentially, the oppressive State and its apparatus uses all at its means to further the interest and benefit of the oppressor. This predator-victim relationship of imperialism, manifest - by way of political domination - in the social, psychological, educational, economic, law enforcement and military realms.[37] The lives and neighborhoods of the

---

[37] SEE: **Towards Colonial Freedom,** by Kwame Nkrumah

oppressed is a very different place than that of the oppressor.[38] The health, educational, cultural concerns and the indisputable human rights of the oppressed are absent! *Compassion is a vacuum in the minds and souls of the oppressor! However, when the oppressed do take on freedom, they will do so without pity and without mercy!*

Hypocritical insensitivity is the template of US foreign policy and this is clearly reflected in the contradiction between the aims of US foreign policy and the lack of **social needs** and **humanitarian development**, the latter two being hallmarks of a genuine civilization.[39]

With a smiling face of deception, media made Obama took the occasion of his first press appearance as president-elect to declare his determination to impose policies of budgetary austerity to contend with a federal deficit for that fiscal year which, according the Congressional Budget Office was exceeding $10.7 trillion. Voicing the neo-liberal interest of the American ruling class and the **"not so hidden hand of Zionism"** that steers US domestic and foreign policy, Obama made clear the intent to eliminate many social programs, and by so doing discount the mass surge of the sixties and early seventies that forced the federal government to implement such reforms. The *"smiling face"* also declared his intent on cost-cutting in the entitlement programs such as Social

---

[38] Franz Fanon, **The Wretched of the Earth**, and see, **A Dying Colonialism**

[39] SEE: **http://www.thirdworldtraveler.com/** (SEE: link; U.S. **Foreign Policy and** .
Pentagon)THIRD WORLD TRAVELER is an archive of articles and book excerpts that seek to tell the truth
about the state of American democracy, media, and foreign policy, and about the impact of the actions of
the United States government, transnational corporations, global trade and financial institutions, and the corporate media, on democracy, social and economic justice, human rights, and war and peace,
in the Third World, and in the developed world.

82

Security, Medicare and Medicaid, callously ignoring the vital importance of such programs to tens of millions of elderly and poor people – with a triple devastating effect on people of color. Out of $10.7 trillion in total federal debt, about 40 percent, or $4.3 trillion, is borrowed from Social Security. The Trust Fund is the largest holder of federal debt, followed by US private investors, who hold $3.4 trillion, and foreign investors, many of them governments, who hold $3 trillion.[40] Obama was willing to steal more from the poor to make the super-rich, even richer. Afghanistan, not counting the additional cost of a doubling of US forces to some 60,000 in Afghanistan. [41]

Manipulating, redirecting, marginalizing, stealing, and maliciously misappropriating the wealth of its mass citizenry in order to accumulate more power, wealth and unjust-capital is *business as usual* for empires. It was done in the imperial conquest of Rome, Persia, Spain, Britain, Germany, Russia, and China and with the current most powerful empire in human history, the united snakes of Amerikkka. Yet, when empires fall they collapse astonishingly quick, the results of an internal and external moral, social, political ideological, and economic malignancy that is a characteristic pathology of systemic evil and injustice – **YOU REAP WHAT YOU SOW AND THE EVIL YOU DO WILL SURELY RETURN UNTO YOUR OWN HOUSE!** The indicators below are just a small list of evidence that the crisis of capitalism and US domestic and foreign policy **is just beginning and Obama has been strategically placed at the helm of a dying ship!**

US foreign Policy with Africa – Part B

---

[40] **wsws.org**

[41] wsws.org

83

Africa: The Passing of the Golden Ages
By John Henrik Clarke (May 1988)
1. The early beginnings

"It can be said with a strong degree of certainty that Africa has had three Golden Ages. The first two reached their climax and were in decline before Europe as a functioning entity in human society was born. Africa's first Golden Age began at the beginning—with the birth of man and the development of organized societies. It is general conceded in most scholarly circles that mankind originated in Africa; this makes the African man the father and the African woman the mother of mankind."

In his book The Progress and Evolution of Man in Africa, Dr. L.S.B. Leakey states that:

"In every country that one visits and where one is drawn into a conversation about Africa, the question is regularly asked, by people who should know better: "But what has Africa contributed to world progress?" The critics of Africa forget that men of science today, with few exceptions, are satisfied that Africa was the birthplace of man himself, and that for many hundreds of centuries thereafter, Africa was in the forefront of all human progress."

Africa's and Africans relationship with Europe, and more specifically the United States, has always been one of contrast, contention and conflict of cultures. For the most part, this relation has been one of people's sovereignty vs. conquest, profiteering and exploration vs. cautious suspicion and repulsion and African humanism vs. categorical anti-humanist predation on the part of empire-quest mentality and ideology of capitalism and US imperialism!

This dialectics of cultures has been the dominant tendency throughout the "Atlantic Slave-trade," the US Civil war and capitalist reconstruction, the balkanizing results of the Berlin Conference of 1884-

84

85, the expansionist foreign policy of the Monroe Doctrine and Manifest Destiny up to the US penetration of Africa and the pursuit of interest in colonialism and neo-colonialism. And, this relationship of inevitable dialectical contention persists and is intensified and rarefied as it reaches the era of civil-war, class struggle and growing people resistance and a growing socialist Revolutionary Pan-African struggle in Africa and the African Diaspora

GLOBAL DISORDER

The Humpty Dumpty of the world capitalist system is the united snakes. The U.S. is the hegemonic power of the G-8 countries and of world imperialism and has the greatest concentration of power, influence and wealth. Around humpty are little eggs – secondary imperialist powers such as Germany, Japan, Britain, France, and Israel. There are even smaller eggs – third rate imperialist powers, such as the Scandinavian countries, Belgian, Switzerland, Austria, Italy, Greece, Spain, Portugal, and Canada. Some of these may even dare call themselves socialist but the essence and material basis of a thing is critical to understand what it is. **It is content and position of the masses in relation to power over society that is essential in determining the degree of socialist development; at the same time, genuine socialism must have a clear and active involvement in the fight against world imperialism and for the development of the socialist world.** There are yet even smaller eggs or sub-imperialist powers such as Mexico, Saudi Arabia, South Africa, Australia, Pakistan, India, Peru, Nigeria, Egypt and a chain of neo-colonial governments and puppet leaders.

Imperialism today is characterized by seizure of land by corruption and war, domestic-colonialism, neo-colonialism, embourgeosiement,[42] seizure of natural resources, exploitation of indigenous labor, geo-political-military spheres of influence, dumping grounds for cheap products, commodity production, surplus labor, alienation of labor, racism, gender oppression, capitalist invasions with genocidal intent, imperialist wars, transfer and delay of metro pole contradictions and a veracious appetite of a diabolical predator. These are the characteristics of the world scope of the U.S. empire in 2011. Its current aims of U.S. imperialism are:

- Controlling the global resources of the earth (Gas, water, oil etc...)
- Creating a new enemy (terrorism and concern for "democracy 'as the reason for intervention and war.
- Increasing a culture of war and domination for conquest and the elimination of any world threat
- Improving classified technologies i.e. Bio Pharmacy, Nanotechnology, Face Recognition Programs and Tracking Chip Devices (implanted, GPS etc...), control Weather and natural forces- Tsunamis, earthquakes, hurricanes as part of a military and control mechanism. The Obama administration with benevolent, promises and illusions provide an ample cover for the beast to survive!

The U.S. led world imperialism of today is vast and powerful; it is a comprehensive world system of oppression and exploitation but imperialism is primarily dependent on Africa, Asia and South America

---

[42] Embourgeosiement (See: Kwame Nkrumah) the argument that, contrary to the class conflict theory of Karl Marx (1818-1883), increasing numbers of what might traditionally be classified as working class people are coming to assume the lifestyle and individualistic values of the so-called middle classes and capitalist system and hence reject in uniting with the masses of the people and in fact resent the working class and have no commitment to collective social and economic goals with the mass of the people. It is the opposite of class consciousness. It is a class position that is much dependent on the maintenance of the imperialist welfare state which itself is dependent primarily on neo-colonialism, especially in Africa.

and their strategic location, resources and people. To the degree that imperialism loses its grip on these areas, it will become destabilized, paralyzed, deprived and mortally wounded. The Black ace Obama card is also part of the U.S. strategy with Africa and Latin America It is with this politico-military strategic thought in mind that Africa and the world must look to development of Revolutionary Pan-Africanism!

THE AFRICA FACTOR

Below is a brief look at the strategic importance of just oil, in just a few African countries. It also shows the workings of neo-colonialism and the need to crush it. As neo-colonialism is attacked and diminished, then to that degree will the crisis within the US and within world imperialism intensify? A clear understanding and definition of neo-colonialism from an Nkrunahist-Toureist perspective is essential. Consider the quotes below:

- ☐ "Survival of the colonial system, in spite of formal recognition of political independence in emerging countries which becomes the victims of an indirect and subtle form of domination by political, economic, social, military or technical means."

(All African people's conference, Cairo March 23-31, 1961; resolution of neo-colonialism, in Colin Legum, Pan-Africanism; a short political guide (London, 1965), p. 254

- ☐ "… An intermediary …the transition belt between the nation and capitalism…that puts on the mask of neo-colonialism".(Franz Fanon, The Wretched of the Earth, p 152)

- ☐ "The essence of neo-colonialism is that the state which is subject to it is in theory independent and has all the outward trappings of international sovereignty. In reality, its economic system and thus its poetical policy is directed from the outside."

(NEO-COLONIALISM IS THE LAST STAGE OF IMPERIALISM)

Nigeria (neo-colonial) Nigeria is the world's sixth-largest exporter of oil and the fifth-largest supplier to the US. Nigeria produces around 3.2 million barrels per day accounting for around eight percent of U.S oil imports. Currently, Nigeria is pumping millions of dollars into parts of the U.S. and the energy capital of the world, Houston, through Chevron, Texaco, ExxonMobil, oil services giant Halliburton (which had U.S Vice President Dick Cheney as CEO). High oil prices brought the Nigerian government $14 billion dollars in 2000. Nigeria has earned $292 billion in oil revenues, according to data compiled by Houston-based PetroGasWorks.com, since the discovery of reserves in 1958 in eastern Nigeria, **with very little to show for uplifting a majority of its people.** "Bonny Light crude" from Nigeria has low-sulphuric content, and is easily converted into gasoline. Nigeria is the only West African country belonging to the Organization of Petroleum Exporting Countries (OPEC). It has been a member of OPEC since 1971, but is now under pressure to withdraw as part of the ongoing effort by the richer countries to drive down the price of raw materials. The US and Israel have been the major backers of this neo-colonial government led by a despicable, ruthless and **a lower than a sewer whole rat** puppet for the US and Israel named **Umaru Musa Yar'Adua.** Similar to US president Obama, he is a puppet of imperialism. When the imperialist and Israel ask them to jump, the only reply is ***How high boss!*** The U.S. has $7.4 billion worth of investment in Nigeria and is planning more. With the realization that oppression brings on resistance and with the growing class struggle and contradiction mounting daily and that they *(imperialist and neo-colonial puppets)* could be imperiled by an unstable Nigeria, the US has sent in forces to train the Nigerian army and police, force(including US- FBI). The US sees Nigeria not just as a source of oil, but also as a regional power that can be used to police tensions in the whole of West Africa. Nigerian troops make up the biggest contingent of the ECOMOG multilateral military force, which has intervened in several countries to put down disturbances and is hope to be a King-pawn in the AFRICOM strategy.

Gabon (neo-colonial)

Omar Ondimba Bongo has been president of Gabon since 1967, and ever since that time he has been a puppet for France, Israel and the US. Gabon has a per capita income four times the average for sub-Saharan Africa, but corruption, neo-colonialism and inequalities in income ensure that a large proportion of the inhabitants are desperately poor. Gabon depended on timber and manganese until oil was discovered offshore in the early 1970s. The oil sector now accounts for 50 percent of GDP, with production in 2001 standing at 301,000 barrels per day. Gabon exports almost half of its commodities to the US, but imports mainly from France. Gabon was formerly a French colony, and is still a member of the CFA (Franc Communauté Financière Africaine). For most of the time since its independence from France, Gabon has been ruled as a one-party puppet state the Gabon Democratic Party (PDG.) The French investigation in the 1990s into the misuse of funds by the Elf oil firm in Gabon caused tensions between Gabon and France. Elf deposited illegal "commissions" in Swiss bank accounts, for the alleged use of top Gabonese politicians.

Like Obama, Omar Ondimba Bongo has a special relation of moral filth with the banks of imperialism and in particular with the Swiss bank.[43]

Republic of Congo (Brazzaville)

---

[43] May 30, 2008 (LPAC)--In late 2006, George Soros, the British empire/Wall Street gatekeeper of the Left, vetted Senator Barack Obama's potential Presidential candidacy on behalf of financier oligarchs. Soros then introduced Obama to a selected financier group, and Obama soon afterwards announced he would seek the White House.

Jacques-**Joachim Yhombi-Opango is president of** Congo Brazzaville, which borders the much bigger Democratic Republic of Congo, and is a substantial oil producer—271,000 barrels per day in 2001. The ruling regime is hoping to benefit from heavy new investment in deep offshore reserves, with production expected to rise to around 400,000 barrels per day. It is backed by the U.S. and France for this reason! Congo Brazzaville was a French colony until 1960, when it became independent and is part of the CFA (The French Monetary system). The government is a thinly disguised dictatorship, which came to power through a bloody military coup in 1997. Its elections have been characterized by flawed electoral rolls, and the main opposition candidates have been barred from standing. The U.S. has had sinister, malicious and ravenousness intentions for the mineral rich and prosperous area of the Congo ever since the U.S. inspired and backed assassination of the great Pan-African combatant and freedom fighter Patrice Lumumba in 1963.[44]

Equatorial Guinea (neo-colonial)
Two puppets of US imperialism

Mr. Obiang Nguema overthrew his uncle, President Francisco Nguema, in 1979. The former leader was tried and executed. *{**Tom fighting Tom over** "**Massa's**" **crumbs}**} Equatorial Guinea's oil production has more than doubled the country's gross national product in three years, having increased from nothing in 1991 to 181,000 barrels per day in 2001. The country was administered by Britain until the middle of the 19th century, and then became a colony of Spain until 1968, when it became independent. President Obiang Nguwma Mbasogo has held power since

---

[44] The New Nation, Bangladesh Independent News Source: CIA releases declassified papers: Assassination plot against Castro, Lumumba uncovered By Xinhua, Washington

August 1979, when he seized power through a military coup. The country has belonged to the CFA since January 1985, and is under French influence. Nevertheless, it was the US oil companies who moved into the country first, and who now dominate its oil industry. But few people have benefited from the oil riches and the country ranks near the bottom of a UN human development index. The corruption watchdog Transparency International[45] has put Equatorial Guinea in the top 10 of its list of corrupt states. Despite calls for more transparency in the sector, President Obiang has said oil revenues are a state secret. He is as deceptive as Obama is on the support he gets from the top capitalist bankers and his ambiguous stimulus plan that gives bankers over 700 billion and cuts basic programs for the needy and poor!

Cameroon and Chad (neo-colonial)

Cameroon produced barrels of oil per day in 2001, down from 88,000 the previous year. This figure is expected to rise to barrels per day by 2010.A tripartite maritime boundary dispute with Equatorial Guinea and Nigeria is currently before the International Court of Justice. _**(Tom fighting Tom over "Massa's" crumbs.)**_ The presence of oil reserves in the Bakassi Peninsula has made all sides determined to hold out for as much of the disputed area as possible. Cameroon is the product of the 1961 unification of what was French Cameroon with part of British Cameroon. It is currently ruled by ethnic-based elite {**colonial tribalism**}. Cameroon is part of the CFA, and much of its trade is with France and Italy. AIDS has become one of the major causes of death in recent years, with over 10 percent of the population infected. [46]Cameroon's neighbor,

---

[45] This is not to say that Transparency International is correct in all its evaluations, but it is "dam sure" correct on this one!- Emphasis by Odinga Mukhtar

[46] www.boydgraves.com/timeline/ See also: Dr. Leonard G. Horowitz, called, *Death in the Air: Globalism, Terrorism and Toxic Warfare.*

the landlocked Chad—another former French colony, in which power is held by an ethnic-based northern elite—is set to start pumping as much as 250,000 barrels a day. Exxon/Mobil is funding the "Chad-Cameroon Development Project," to develop oilfields in southern Chad. In order to export the crude oil from the country's landlocked oilfields, it will be transported approximately 1,070 kilometers (663 miles) by underground pipeline to a marine terminal on the coast of Cameroon. Billions of dollars are now being pumped into sub-Saharan Africa, one of the poorest areas of the world. This money is primarily going towards capital development connected with draining the country of its vital resource. For example, the best roads are those that are used in the development of the oil industry. The population suffers from famine and disease on a scale that can only be considered a crime in the 21st century. The capitalist West has made much – "bull-shit ado" of the transition to "democratically elected governments in Africa," but in countries with such a stark division between rich and poor forked tong talk of democracy has little meaning for the mass of the population. It only serves to conceal a new grab for Africa's resources resembling that which took place in the 19th century, with profit-hungry companies claiming the right to exploit vast areas of territory at the expense of the local population.

In W.E.B. Du Bois' classic work, *"The World and Africa,"* the point is convincingly made that **the most significant piece of real estate in the word is the continent of Africa!** Not only was Africa the birth place of humankind, but the natural resources and the people of Africa have been vital for all empires and is certainly vital for the empire ambitions of U.S. capitalism. This point has been stated throughout the book. We have already made the point of the strategic importance of Africa with regards to oil, but oil is only one of the vital natural resources within the bosom of the continent of Africa. Oil is only one of the life sustaining mineral resources that lie in the womb of mother Africa and oil is only one of the resources that can be used in a **"strategic political-military sense",** just one of a proliferation of resources that can be

92

leverage to affect policy within the cities of the Diaspora and African communities of the Diaspora. **Here the political coordination on a Revolutionary Pan-African basis can be decisive in holding back the fangs of a barbaric police state and/or a factor in critically persuading a technology driven and profit defending US military that their policy and strategy will certainly be at a cost of losing access to a vital resource needed to drive the engines and hard drives a its military machine!**

Next to oil, one could speak on the strategic significance of the mineral Colton. Many would find it hard to imagine and many would be in unconscious denial if they were told that, computer technology cell phones and even the latest Play Station and all video games sold in the US and around the world are dependent on and tainted with the blood of 3.2 million African deaths since 1998. Many would find it hard to imagine and many would be in unconscious denial that much of the U.S. high tech armed forces were also dependent on the same horrific statistics of millions African deaths. Yet because of a backward educational system, a racist and controlled media and legacies of domestic colonial unconsciousness, many are not aware of the strategic significance of the proliferation of African natural resources, particularly one termed Colton. Nor are they aware of the political-military strategic potential of revolutionary pan-African organization and control of the resources of Mother-Farther Africa.

The mineral Colton is the plasma of high tech, and it is high tech (computer industry) that is the essential required nutrient that insure the health of the politically and culturally pathology that is known as modern capitalism. Without the mineral Colton organic decomposition and mortality would come soon to modern industry and capitalism. This one mineral is that essential to industry and to the modern "high tech" US armed forces which is a computer driven weapon of mass destruction of much of the world humanity.

The minerals columbium and tantalite, or Colton for short is a rare, hard and dense metal, very resistant to corrosion and high temperatures and is an excellent electricity and heat conductor. It is used in the microchips of cell phone batteries to prolong duration of the charge, making this business flourish. Provisions for just 2004 had foreseen sales of 1,000 million units. To these properties are added that its extraction does not entail heavy costs --it is obtained by digging in the mud (in other word the use of cheap African labor gives a cheap labor force that produces enormous profits.) and that it is easily sold, enabling the companies involved in the business to obtain juicy dividends.

Even though Colton is extracted in Brazil, Thailand and much of it from Australia --the prime producer of Colton on a world level-- it is in Africa where 80% of the world reserves are to be found. Within this continent, the Democratic Republic of Congo concentrates over 80% of the deposits, where 10,000 miners toil daily in the province of Kivu (eastern Congo), a territory that has been occupied since 1998 by the armies of Rwanda and Uganda. A series of companies has been set up in the zone, associated to large transnational capital, local governments and military forces (both state and "guerrilla") in a dispute over the control of the region for the extraction of Colton and other minerals.

If the Colton on the Congo was controlled entirely by a Revolutionary Pan- African entity, such a positive force could not only dictate to imperialist powers but would be a formidable force that could by its conscious denial, crumble every major center of capitalism along with their industries and high-tech armies. The US needs Colton like our bodies need a pumping heart.

Below From Axioms **of Kwame Nkrumah**

- "It has often been said that Africa is poor," what nonsense! It is not Africa that is poor, it is the Africans, who are impoverished by centuries of exploitation and domination

- In a revolutionary situation, it is a crime against the people to forgive those who have betrayed them

- Neo-colonialism has no permanent friends; its only companions are its own interests.

- The economic-military-strategic significance of just "SOME"

Of the resources of Africa

Consider the research and data obtained from brother Junior Ricardo Stanton;[*]

"Africa accounts for a significant proportion of U.S. imports-100% of industrial diamonds; 58% of uranium;48% of cocoa; 44% of manganese used in producing steel, 40% of antimony to harden metals; 39% of platinum, 36% of cobalt for jet engines and high strength alloys, 33% of petroleum, 30% of beryl used in weapons and nuclear reactors, 23% of chromite used in gun barrels, 21 % columbium-tantalum for heat resisting alloys in missiles and rockets and 21% of coffee," from Imperialism and Dependency Obstacles to African Development by Daniel A. Offiong.

Once while I was giving a talk about Africa to a group of

---

[*] The Theft Of African Wealth
By Junious Ricardo Stanton
http://assatashakur.org/forum/showthread.php?p=50695

adolescent African-American males a young brother asked, "If Africa is so rich in natural resources, why do the people look so poor and starving?" Due to time constraints, I didn't have enough minutes to explain why, aside from racist anti-African stereotyping, the mass media deliberately depicts Africans as under developed, destitute, backward, diseased and staving. I didn't have time to tell them about the Berlin Conference of 1884 in which 14 European nation states including the United States sat around a large table and carved up the continent conspiring to shanghai its riches, its natural and human resources and plotting to appropriate them for their benefit.

Even today, most Africans in America think Africa is underdeveloped because our people are not as intelligent, technologically advanced or sophisticated as Europeans or Asians. Most of our people think Afrikans are starving because they are too lazy or too backward to invent efficient labor-saving devices. Given we have been lied to about African history and European history we never stop to ask how the roles and fortunes of the two land masses get reversed in just five hundred years?

We don't question how Europe went from being a resource less, backward, starving, disease ridden and destitute subcontinent to commandeering most of the world's wealth while Africa went from being the cradle of civilization with most of the gold, rich lands and mineral resources to being a vast expanse of arrested social and technological development?

Even before the industrial and technological revolutions, European imperialism and colonialism created wealth generating opportunities and improved the quality of life throughout Europe while simultaneously introducing disease, social disruption, death, ecological and trade

96

unbalances everywhere they set foot on planet earth. This was true no matter which European nation was involved. Not to mention how the whites forced or attempted to force the indigenous inhabitants of the lands they invaded or the millions they kidnapped or bartered for around the globe to work for."

Finally, allow me to add more proof of the strategic significance of the resources of Africa by sharing data obtained from the conscious research of our Pan-African warrior, Brother Roy Walker. I am greatly indebted and appreciative of the info sent to me on this indispensable topic and of the information from his web site. (For web site info contact: RWalker949@aol.com

"The material wealth of Africa is absolutely phenomenal. In this message, we will consider just a handful of the major commodities produced in Africa (cobalt, manganese, chromium, gold, cocoa, palladium and platinum), which due to the contemporary political economic configuration of Africa, and her place in the distorted global political economy, really does not and cannot benefit the great majority of African people(s). Note that I have not included such valuable assets as uranium, Colton, diamonds, vanadium and tanzanite, oil and gas, coffee, cotton, tea, fisheries, edible oils, timber, coal and so on.

I.   Military uses of strategic metals...

"... In 1975 the United States imported $12 billion in nonfuel minerals. By 1980 the figure was up to $29 billion and is expected to reach $85 billion by the years 2000."

The availability of these minerals have an extremely important impact on American industry and in turn, on U.S. defense capabilities. Without just a few critical minerals, such as cobalt, manganese, chromium, and platinum, it would be virtually impossible to produce many defense products such as jet engine, missile components, electronic components, iron, steel, etc. The severity of the problem becomes more apparent when the location of these minerals is considered. Virtually all the worlds' reserves of some strategic minerals lie either in the (former) Soviet Union or in Africa. Between them, these two areas contain over 90% of the world platinum, manganese and chromium ores..."

This section is designed to analyze these minerals to determine the impact on the U.S. if the normal supply of any of them were disrupted.

Only four will be discussed (chromium, cobalt, manganese and platinum) because the majority of the free world reserves of each is located in Africa, each has a major impact on the U.S. economy, and the U.S. imports a majority of its needs from Africa."

"**Chromium** is a white, crystalline, very hard metallic chemical with a very high resistance to corrosion. It is used in alloys required in stainless steel, tool steel, and high-temperature applications. It is also used in jet aircraft engines and aircraft structural members and areas of high skin friction. Of the total chromite consumed, the metallurgical industry uses 63%, the refractory industry 17%, and the chemical industry 24%." " Since 1961, the U.S. has relied on foreign sources for 100% of its chromium needs. Major concentrations of chromium are in Africa, with the largest known reserves in the Republic of South Africa and the purest grades are in Zimbabwe. These two countries together account for 98% of the world's reserves." The extent to which other minerals can be substituted for chromium is quite limited. There is no material which can adequately replace chrome in the steel industry and no substitutes exist for its aerospace industry and no substitutes exist for its aerospace applications. In a crisis, some consumers of chromium could continue to function by reducing their usage of the mineral. However, most critical industries, particularly defense, could not continue to operate without

98

normal supplies." Due to the lack of substitutes, the limited capability of industry to operate without chromium, and the minerals concentration in South Africa and Zimbabwe, the U.S. would be forced to draw extensively from the defense stockpile in the event of a supply disruption. The stockpile could meet domestic needs for up to three years. Therefore, the U.S. is capable of meeting any short-term disruption of its chromium supply but does not have sufficient alternate sources in the event the production of either Zimbabwe or South Africa were permanently lost."

" **Cobalt** is a hard, silver-gray metal which closely resembles both iron and nickel in hardness, strength and other properties. It is used as a high-temperature, high-strength alloy agent in stationary gas turbine and jet engines. It is also used in magnetic alloys in electronic equipment."

"Because domestic production cannot compete with the price of foreign sources, no cobalt has been mined in the U.S. since 1971. Increases in the price of cobalt or severe reductions in its availability would be required before domestic production could be profitable."

"Four countries in Africa possess 52% of the free world's reserves: Zaire, Zambia, Morocco, and Botswana. Loss of the output from Zambia, Morocco, or Botswana would have a critical impact on the marketplace. However, Zaire produces over 60% of the free world's cobalt of which the U.S. purchases 65% of its needs. A loss of Zaire's cobalt would have a drastic impact on the United States."

"Some substitution can be made using nickel and chromium. However, 50 to 60 percent of the cobalt consumed is essential in high-temperature alloys for jet engines and steam turbines. In the event of a shortage, industry will not be able to drastically cut back on its uses of cobalt without a serious impact on U.S. defense requirements. About 70% of U.S. consumption of cobalt is used in alloys that will not tolerate substitutes." " Because the use of cobalt plays a significant part in both industrial and military applications, and with limited substitutes available, the U.S. must ensure an adequate source in the event of supply disruptions. Other foreign sources may offset a minor shortfall, but a total loss of Zaire's cobalt would have serious consequences to the U.S."

Current Strategy of US Capitalism Regarding Africa

NEPAD & AFRICOM: A Case Study in Neo-colonialism

The New Partnership for Africa's Development (**NEPAD**) and U.S. Africa Command, or **AFRICOM**, are the latest attempts of the US to re-colonize Africa, by way of puppet regimes and proxy African armies. It is a strategy based on neo-colonialism, internal corruption. The deception comes in the form of a "Black" face. In a time of cultural and racial integrity to be Black is necessary but it ***"DAM SURE is not sufficient!"*** **African people must realize that we must fight and destroy the reactionary elements within our culture while we at the same time, wage a relentless offensive against the external enemy.**

"The mechanisms of neo-colonialism. It is necessary to study, understand, expose and actively combat neo-colonialism, for their methods are subtle and varied..."

Neo-Colonialism, the Last Stage of imperialism, by Kwame Nkrumah

AFRICOM & NEO-COLONIALISM

What is AFRICOM?

AFRICOM was the distorted brainchild (an Omen-child) of the U.S. ruling class by way of the George W. Bush administration and according to pentagon-Speak, Africa Command (AFRICOM) not only
100

places oil and global military strategy as the number one and two goals of America's Africa policy but places the State Department's assistance program for Africa firmly under Pentagon control. It was created on October 1, 2007, and as I have briefly explained with just a short analysis and review of US foreign policy, nothing of any good to humanity or true people's liberty has ever come out of the Pentagon, the strategic think and planning center of the awesome but reprehensible us military!

AFRICOM, a weapon of empire initiated by the Bush administration is currently being carried on by the Obama administration. Initially AFRICOM was a sub-unified command under the European Command (EUCOM) in Stuttgart, Germany. On October 1, 2008, AFRICOM became a separate unified command. AFRICOM is still looking for a permanent base in Africa but there is likelihood that it will be scattered as a "distributed command" across the continent to further extend America's military presence and oppressive might into every region of Africa. Comparable to America's contempt for Africa people (Black people) in the U.S. and the Diaspora, U.S. foreign policy has never operated in the best interest of African people nor Africa's best interest and analogous to the U.S. empire quest it has always been an abhorrence and a resounding arch-enemy to African culture!

"STUPID IS AS STUPID DOES "

The militarism of America's policy on Africa centers on propping up dictators and Black puppets who have bought into the globalization agenda us imperialism and who have offered up their souls, governments, armies and land bases for the U.S. military incursion into Africa, an incursion that seeks to recolonize the continent. The militarization of U.S. Africa policy is highlighted by the fact that Agency for International Development (USAID) [closely linked to CIA covert activities in Africa and elsewhere] and State Department officials are to be assigned to the AFRICOM headquarters. AFRICOM current commander and "US Army

101

General William E. "Kip" Ward – **a twin puppet to Obama**; will be assisted by military and State Department Foreign Service deputies. As with the top militaristic foreign policy "expert" in the Bush administration, Frazer, an African American, the selection of Ward, also an African American, is a shameless attempt by the Obama administration and US ruling class to mask the true intent of AFRICOM among Africa's and the Diaspora's Black population.

Along with being *the "Fort Apache"* of US militarism in Africa, it is the US's intent that AFRICOM serve as a major pass-through for U.S. covert operations in Africa, mainly because U.S. civilian assistance funds will be funneled through AFRICOM's budget, and, therefore, be controlled by the Pentagon. The funding mechanisms for AFRICOM will also permit private military contractors like Backwater USA, DynCorp, and Triple Canopy, Bechtel, Halliburton and more to extend their operations in Africa and for Zionism to expand its morally filthy hand even more in Africa's internal affairs. It is clear that the Necons are planning to turn Africa into the next war zone by providing military aid for the crushing of secessionist, tribal, and democracy and liberation movements in Africa. We see U.S. military, CIA, FBI and law enforcement-providing intelligence and weapons that are now being used against political protesters, freedom fighters and revolutionaries in Kenya, Ethiopia, Somalia, Ghana, and Guinea and wherever the clutches of the imperialist beast can grab a hold. (See chart of US military plans for Africa by way of AFRICOM)

ONLY A UNIFIED REVOLUTIONARY PAN-AFRIVA STRATEGY CAN DEFEAT IMPERIALISM

{See: Kwame Nkrumah: Africa Must unite, Kwame Nkrumah: neo-Colonialism the last Stage of Imperialism, Dr. Kwame Ture: OSAGYEFO'S VISION, INEVITABLE REALITY:

AFRICA WILL BE FREE . . . UNIFIED AND SOCIALIST

Neo-colonialism comes in many forms and faces, but the essence and result are all the same:

BAD NEWS FOR AFRICA   AND AFRICAN PEOPLE

According to many sources "(The New Partnership for African Development) is his brainchild of former president of South Africa President Thabo Mbeki - *a traitor to African people*

WHAT IS NEPAD? The New Partnership for Africa's Development (NEPAD) is a vision and strategic framework by the US for the subjugation and control of Africa's resources, strategic location and for the exploitation and oppression of African people on the continent. Partnership with imperialism, the World Bank, the IMF and reaction can and never will lead to any genuine development and certainly not Africa's development. NEPAD is a neo-liberal subterfuge and a three card molly trick of capitalism, Zionism and imperialism.

THE ORIGINS

The NEPAD strategic framework document arises from a mandate given to the five initiating Heads of State (Algeria, Egypt, Nigeria, Senegal, and South Africa) by the Organization of African Unity (OAU) to develop an integrated socio-economic development framework for Africa. The 37th Summit of the OAU in July 2001 formally adopted the strategic framework document. The deception and *"rip off"* of NEPAD is seen in the analysis of it origin. The OAU far from being the vehicle for Africa unity and development has - **for the most part** – been in control of African reactionaries. Initially the OAU according to its original charter was to be the basis of African continental unity. This was Kwame Nkrumah's and genuine Revolutionary Pan-Africanist intentions. In reality, the OAU like the current African Union is primarily control by the clutches of neo-colonialism and their puppets, notwithstanding the progressive and revolutionary forces that are a part of it, who are a small but conscious minority. On this point Kwame Ture was very clear in his

"OSAGYEFO'S VISION, INEVITABLE REALITY: AFRICA WILL BE LIBERATED, UNIFIED AND SOCIALIST

Also see: Kwame Nkrumah's Africa Must Unite and Sekou Toure's, The United States of Africa.

"Africa is the richest continent in the world. Africans wherever you find them are among the poorest people in the world. This contradiction can be explained in one word - imperialism. The worldwide poverty of Africans is the result of brutal racist exploitation, slavery, and colonialism. To resolve this contradiction Africa must be totally liberated, unified and socialist. After twenty-five (25) years of independence certain truths are undeniable. We must quickly eliminate all confusion on the question of the first step towards progress - economic or political. The problem is an ideological one of immense proportions which calls for rigorous struggle. At a minimum level, it demands a clear understanding of what is progress, buildings or human relations. Capitalism does not just seek to plunder our resources and labor, it also seeks to limit our thinking." See: Dr. Kwame Ture; **Osagefo's Vision**

Racist imperialism, which everywhere tries to impose inferiority complexes on us, would have us think that in order to make progress we must "catch up" with the unplanned monstrosities of London, Paris or New York. Some, so contaminated with this fatal disease, think that unless our village has at least one mini skyscraper we have not made progress. ALL conscious Africans treat this calumny with the contempt it deserves. Who, having the slightest understanding of history, can question the African s ability to construct, when the pyramids still stands! We cannot understand those who think progress equals western cities and life-styles.

The course taken by reactionary regimes in Africa has clearly demonstrated that this is not the path to progress. These regimes to "catch up" with the "developed world" have put an immense burden on future generations; thus, demonstrating their total irresponsibility! It is only human nature that each generation seeks to ameliorate conditions for future generations. Since independence we have seen this path is anti-human.

Such terms as developed, underdeveloped and developing nation are euphemistically used to cover exploitation. Indeed. the term developed nation is one we should never seek to realize. Something developed has reached a final stage. Humanity instinctively seeks limitless progress.

Geographical space is limited. A given country after having arranged its physical space in a given time in harmony with its ideology may call itself developed. Our thinking is not limited to space or time; it transcends them! When we speak of progress in a society, it is not just the material aspect of life but more importantly the immaterial aspects, the values for example which demonstrate the true understanding of human nature and the role of woman and man in society to take more than they give or give more than they take.

Those who thought a politically divided Africa could speak of economic development on any level must admit of Osagyefo's clear-sighted vision when the International Monetary Fund and The World Bank wish to make it appear as if Africa, from whom European capitalist countries have plundered too many human and material resources, owes them anything.

This is a tragic joke! It is to Africa's stolen people and wealth that they owe their "development." Qsagyefo told us long ago, "seek ye first the political kingdom."

From **OSAGYEFO'S VISION, INEVITABLE REALITY: AFRICA WILL BE LIBERATED, UNIFIED AND SOCIALIST**, by Dr. Kwame Ture{formerly Stokely Carmichael

NEPAD was initially met with a great deal of skepticism from much of civil society in Africa as playing into the "Washington Consensus". The term **Washington Consensus,** was initially coined in 1989 by John Williamson to describe a set of ten specific economic policy prescriptions that he considered to constitute a "standard" reform package promoted for crisis-wracked developing countries by Washington D.C based institutions such as the International Monetary Fund (IMF), World Bank and the U.S. Treasury Department.[1]

Subsequently, as Williamson himself has pointed out, the term has come to be used in a different and broader sense, as a synonym for market fundamentalism; in this broader sense, Williamson states, it has been criticized by writers such as George Soros and Nobel Laureate Joseph E. Stiglitz.[2] The Washington Consensus is also criticized by others such as some Latin American politicians and heterodox economists. The term has become associated with neoliberal policies in general and drawn into the broader debate over the expanding role of the free market, constraints upon the state, and US influence on other countries' national sovereignty. The U.S. and othet neo-liberals hold up NEPAD as a model of economic development. The contradiction should be obvious to any who are
"consciously" African centered and/or conscious period; This is to say, who the hell is the U.S. to be an example in the first place. In July 2002, members of some forty African social movements, trade unions, youth and women's organizations, NGOs, religious organizations and others endorsed the African Civil Society Declaration on rejecting NEPAD; a similar hostile view was taken by African scholars and activist intellectuals in the 2002 Accra Declaration on Africa's Development Challenge—Adopted at end of Joint CODESRIA-TWN-AFRICA

Conference on Africa's Development Challenges in the Millennium, Accra 23-26 April 2002.

Part of the problem in this rejection was the process by which NEPAD was adopted was insufficiently participatory -- civil society was almost totally excluded from the discussions by which it came to be adopted. The poor quality of the actual NEPAD document is to some extent a reflection of this lack of consultation. Consequently, The origin and focus of NEPAD was and is essentially, "elitist." Shame on Thabo Mbeki, but elitism is nothing new for the African National Congress! More recently, NEPAD has also been criticized by some of its initial backers, who accused NEPAD of wasting hundreds of millions of dollars and achieving nothing.– Like many other intergovernmental bodies, NEPAD suffers from slow decision-making, and a relatively poorly resourced and often cumbersome implementing framework. There is a great lack of information about the day to day activities of the NEPAD secretariat -- the website is notably uninformative -- that does not help its case.

To even survive empires must have the critical nutrition of controlled or occupied land, overpowering and exploitation of a people and the rape and pillage of their resources notwithstanding, the necessity of the former for expansion and super profits! Yet, this very fact will lead to the demise of empires. A moral truism captured in the words of Fredrick Douglas, *"The limits of tryants are prescribed by the endurance of those whom they oppressed."*

"The path of the righteous man is beset on all sides by the iniquities of the selfish and the tyranny of evil men. Blessed is he who, in the name of charity and good will, shepherds the weak through the valley of the darkness. For he is truly his brother's keeper and the finder of lost children. And I will strike down upon thee with great vengeance and furious anger those who attempt to poison and destroy my brothers. And you will know I am the Lord when I lay my vengeance upon you."

Ezekiel 25:17

Chapter Four

BEYOND US IMPERIALISM AND OBAMA DRAMA: "OUR FREEDOM LIES IN A STRONG AFRICA AND COMMUNITY POWER."

"That only a Revolutionary mass, Pan African Socialist Party can achieve true African unification is an objective fact not a subjective wish by the Osagyefo. A cursory glance at Africans' centuries - long struggle with its rich and diversified experiences and thanks to Osagyefo's work, insures the fulfillment of this prerequisite for total liberation. The struggle for a unified, socialist Africa has been raging though undetected by many. This demand by the masses will soon gush forth the hurricane, which has built up since the "winds of change" of the 50's. Osagyefo's vision will be inevitable reality. No force on earth can stop Africa. She will be totally liberated, unified and socialist."

Osagyefo's Vision, by Kwame Ture

In his book, Neo-Colonialism the Last Stage of Imperialism, Kwame Nkrumah makes it clear that one of the last battle ground for imperialism will be in Africa, where imperialism will find its inevitable death!   He also says, {"A determined attack must be made on the entrenched position of the minority reactionary elements amongst our own peoples. For the dramatic exposure in recent years of the nature and extent of the class struggle in Africa, through the succession of reactionary military coups and the outbreak of civil wars, particularly in West and Central Africa, has demonstrated the unity between the interests of neocolonialism and the indigenous bourgeoisie." *Class Struggle in Africa:* The US strategy for Africa and its use of reactionary puppets in domestic and foreign policy is doomed to failure; this is not only true for Africa but , Iraq, Lebanon, Afghanistan, Columbia, the U.S. and wherever the voucher of U.S. imperialism and Zionism chooses to fly or roost! Yes! Capitalism, Zionism and imperialism have caused the underdevelopment of Africa but the rise of African to world dominance and influence must assuredly lead to the decline and foreseeable death of imperialism AND THANK GOD AND GOOD RIDENCE!

"I referred to some of Obama's ideas which point to his role in a system that denies every principle of justice. Some throw their hands up in horror if anything is said to criticize the important personality, even if it is done with decency and respect. This is usually accompanied by subtle and not so subtle darts from those with the means to throw and transform them into the elements of media terror imposed on the peoples to sustain the unsustainable."

Reflections by Comrade Fidel

CONTRADICTIONS BETWEEN OBAMA'S POLITICS AND ETHICS

This fourth and final chapter will speak to suggested solutions and alternatives to the Obama Drama - in other words - if not capitalism, if not US neo-liberalism and neo-colonialism, if not oppression then what? Marcus Garvey said that when all else fails, "conditions will make us organize"!

"I AGREE WITH NKRUMAH, PAN-AFRICANISM IS THE SOLUTION TO THE PROBLEMS OF PEOPLE OF AFRICA DESCENT."

From Malcolm X Speaks

"We shall measure our progress by the improvement in the health of our people; by the number of children in school, and by the quality of their education; by the availability of water and electricity in our towns and villages, and by the happiness which our people take in being able to manage their own affairs. The welfare of our people is our chief pride, and it is by this that my Government will ask to be judged."

Dr. Kwame Nkrumah, "Broadcast to the Nation," 24, December 1957

In past chapters, I have tried to show the real meaning of the strategy of deception that is contained in the orchestrated frenzy of the Obama campaign, the election of Barack Obama, the Obama administration, the policies mouth by Obama and the domestic and foreign policy of the US in its' current phase of neo-liberalism and empire decline.

Constructive criticism must at least attempt to offer corrective

111

actions and solutions, and revolutionary consciousness demands such. Consequently, this fourth and final chapter will speak to suggested solutions and alternatives to the Obama Drama - in other words - if not capitalism, if not US neo-liberalism and neo-colonialism, if not oppression then what? Marcus Garvey said that when all else fails, "conditions will make us organize"! **Organize or perish!** In the short and long run, the only solution to the political-social and economic problems of African people lies with the context of the African Revolution! Revolution is a social-political phenomenon that proceeds in a dialectical pattern, that is to say ***conscious organized quantity must be built and made to lead to conscious organized quality.*** Revolutionary struggle is a process that does not move in a straight line; it is not an event but a series of strategic stages and stages of transition with varying modes of struggle moving through periods of reform, turbulence, "apparent" stagnation, rapid movement, flows and ebbs and always much struggle.

The Worldwide African Revolution is certainly no exception to the laws of development. It is critical to know what to do under a given set of circumstances and how to best move the historical dynamic forward. An imperative in this regards is ideology - "correct ideology" - , strategy, organization, cadre development and mass development- leadership and involvement! Action without thought is blind and thought without action is empty!

BRIEF SUMMARIES OF CHAPTERS ONE, TWO AND THREE

The following are very brief summaries - by way of bullet points - of the first three chapters, which are crucial in an understanding of this final essay which seeks to offer some ideas towards an alternative and solution

Chapter One- Obama Drama: Neo-Colonial Deception & Intrigue

Neo-colonialism is essentially a strategy of deception. In the Obama case, capitalism (finance capital) and White racist ruling

112

*class power- by way of the US government - gives the false impression of Black control, Black Power or real people power. In reality, finance capital maintains control–politically and economically–and also controls the strings of a puppet leadership that give a semblance and lip service to democratic concerns and populist interest, but in reality, it is the same old **"oppression as usual!"***

☐ Obama's unquestionable political allegiance to his ideological and financial sponsors argues in a tenaciously and culturally embarrassing way for a person that has betrayed his people, prostituted his ethics, and as Franz Fanon points out in, "Pitfalls of National Consciousness"[47], shows Obama to be a willing instrument of his people's own oppression

☐ Obama is nothing more than the mouth piece for a forked tongue domestic and foreign policy and a deceptive mask that will seek to trick many in Africa, the African community and the world into accepting US strategy, US military, US intrigue, US capitalism and US neo-colonialism. How can you be for the little person and at the same time tenaciously being for the oppressors of the people?

☐ If politics makes strange bed fellows, then Obama has amassed a curious assemble of sleep around partner- particularly morally filthy Zionist bed fellows.

☐ Obama is merely the product of a right wing and heavily influenced Zionist grooming process and effective marketing campaign which has utilized media savvy and technology to sell this new version of a very old product - the Democratic Party "friend of the people," - previously disgustingly

---

[47] Franz Fanon, <u>The Wretched of the Earth</u>

incarnated in the "insurgent" candidacy of Jimmy Carter in 1976, then in the "man from Hope," Bill Clinton himself, in 1992 and now, the misleading smiling face of Obama.

☐ Although many Africans – especially those in the US – "went crazy" for Obama, most voted and supported him based on emotions and aspirations of change. Whereas I understand the emotions and the aspirations, Obama's aspirations are not the aspirations of his people.

☐ The financial backers and major promoters of the Obama presidential campaign and the Obama presidency are some of the most racist right-wing elements in the world.

☐ *OBAMA IS A STRETGY OF NEO-LIBERAL AND NEO-COLONIAL DECEPTION!*

Chapter Two: The Domestic Strategy of American neo-liberal Ruling class (The Class Struggle)

☐ "Class struggle is a fundamental theme of recorded history. In every non-socialist society, there are two main categories of class, the ruling class or classes, and the subject class or classes. The ruling class possesses the major instruments of economic production and distribution, and the means of establishing its political domination, {**including the US presidency**}[48] while the subject class serves the interests of the ruling class, and is politically, economically and socially dominated by it. There is conflict between the ruling class and the exploited class. The nature and cause of the conflict is influenced by the development of productive forces. That is, in any given class formation, whether it be feudalism, capitalism, or any other type of society, the institutions and ideas associated with it arise from the level of

---

[48] Emphasis added by Odinga Mukhtar

114

productive forces and the mode of production. The moment private ownership of the means of production appears, and capitalists start exploiting workers the capitalists become a bourgeois class, the exploited workers a working class. For in the final analysis, a class is nothing more than the sum total of individuals bound together by certain interests who as a class they try to preserve and protect."[49]

☐

The US presidency has always been a mass deception. American capitalism and imperialism is controlled by those who own and control the major means of production. Those who think that one man or a president controls the US economy and government are fooled as much as a child believing in an Easter Bunny and a White- or Black Santa Claus coming down the chimney. {See: **Who Rules America: by G. William Domhoff; Also see:** The Rich and the Super-Rich: A Study in the Power of Money Today: **by** Ferdinand Lundberg.}

☐ **Obama condemned reparations**

☐ Obama's cabinet is a roll call of Zionist and supporters of the illegitimate and immoral government of Israel

---

[49] Kwame Nkrumah, <u>Class Struggle in Africa</u>

- One cannot be pro-Israel and pro Black at the same time. The two are in total contradiction

- Obama condemned the world conference on racism.

- Obama has supported most of the Bush foreign policy

Chapter three: US Foreign policy and neo-liberalism- The Africa strategy

- The global reach of the United States is backed by its' foreign policy by which the United States interacts with foreign nations. US foreign policy from 1776 to present, in general - and specifically in relation to Africa - has been a policy and strategy of invasions, destabilizations, assassinations, State sponsored terror, deception, orchestrated coup de tau, (media, NGO and organizational manipulation), resource pillage, oppression, exploitation, murder, underdevelopment, terror and a forked tong diplomacy, backed by a gun boat-air assault and infantry perverse persuasion, " currently financed by an over 13 trillion dollar economy and the new mouth of US imperialism, **Obama** , a puppet that is seeking to increase the military budget as he calls for billions more to bail out the super-rich!

☐ The foreign policy of the US, in this beginning of a new presidency in 2009, will only follow the path of the treacherous legacy that birthed this country, a tale of genocidal assault on the indigenous of the Western hemisphere, the oppressive utilization of Asian labor, the exploitation of White workers, and the enslavement of the African. **YOU CAN NOT BE A GOOD PRESIDENT OF AN EVIL EMPIRE!**

☐ Africa's and Africans relationship with Europe, and more specifically the United States, has always been one of contrast, contention and conflict of cultures. For the most part, this relation has been one of people's sovereignty vs. conquest, profiteering and exploration vs. cautious suspicion and repulsion and African humanism vs. categorical anti-humanist predation on the part of empire-quest mentality and ideology of capitalism and US imperialism! [50]

☐ Not only was Africa the birth place of humankind, but the natural resources and the people of Africa have been vital for all empires and is certainly vital for the empire ambitions of US capitalism. This point has been stated throughout the book. We have already made the point of the strategic importance of Africa with regards to oil, but oil is only one of the vital natural resources within the bosom of the continent of Africa. Oil is only one of the life sustaining mineral resources that lie in the womb of mother Africa and oil is only one of the resources that can be used in a **"strategic political-military sense,"** **for the liberation of Africa and humanity!**

---

[50] Walter Rodney, How Europe Underdeveloped Africa; Also, Kwame Nkrumah, Neo-Colonialism: The Last Stage of Imperialism

☐ "Africa accounts for a significant proportion of U.S. imports-100% of industrial diamonds; 58% of uranium;48% of cocoa; 44% of manganese used in producing steel, 40% of antimony to harden metals; 39% of platinum, 36% of cobalt for jet engines and high strength alloys, 33% of petroleum, 30% of beryl used in weapons and nuclear reactors, 23% of chromite used in gun barrels, 21 % columbium-tantalum for heat resisting alloys in missiles and rockets and 21% of coffee," from Imperialism and Dependency Obstacles to African Development by Daniel A. Offiong.

SO WHAT IS THE ALTERNATIVE AND COURSE OF POSITIVE ACTION?

We stand on the shoulders of the giants that came before us. In my view, much of the solutions to our current problems are in the ideologies, efforts, legacies, experiences and strategies of our {African} glorious history. In making these suggestions of an alternative and solutions, I am not so foolish as to offer them as my ideas. Perhaps my wording and expressions, but certainly not my ideas. I am indebted to the **"masse of the people- especially the courageous African masses"** the people are the genuine makers of history and in particular , I am indebted to the ideology of Nkrumahism-Tourism, the great   Revolutionary Pan-Africanist, and my years of experience and learning while in the All African People Revolutionary Party (AAPRP) and the current AAPRP-GC (GC meaning HQ in Guinea Conakry). **PLEASE NOTE THAT I DO NOT CLAIM TO SPEAK OFFICIALLY FOR THE AAPRP-GC, AS THIS WRITING REFLECTS MY INDIVIDUAL VIEWS!**

"OUR FREEDOM LIES IN A STRONG AFRICA AND COMMUNITY POWER."

"I began revolution with 82 men. If I had to do it again, I'd do it with 10 or 15 and absolute faith. It does not matter how small you are, if you have faith and plan of action."

"As a revolutionary, I am a force of nature"

Fidel Castro

"To contemplate the building of community power in the US, organizational development and we must view the struggle in the U.S. as revolutionary struggle not in isolation of the world struggle – and for African people particularly, the world-wide Africa struggle; not to do so would be more than myopic, it would be disastrous and downright stupid!"

At this time (2011) when US imperialism is playing its {**Black Ace card**} internationally and domestically, the US also is in a pre-revolutionary crisis. A pre-revolutionary crisis period and stage is where the oppressed are in a situation where the oppressor (the enemy) has overwhelming control. This is known as a zone under enemy control.; yet in this state of affairs-due to the increasing oppression, growing police state, deteriorating political—economic-social conditions of the people along with the people's growing distrust and disappointment with the government - the potential for mass unrest and resistance is a time bomb with a very short fuse! An excellent example of this stage is the current condition of the African in America and Europe and many places in the world where our people are. We can see this in the mass upsurge of youth and workers in North Africa, the Caribbean, Asia and even Austria. Open mass residence to oppression and neo-liberalism is the trend in the world today. In the U.S. the immediate tasks that the people, must address in their day to day struggle and work, especially within the strategic context of building a Revolutionary Pan-African struggle is organization

119

involvement, core cadre development, organizational networking and joint organization programs leading towards coalitions and the building of an African united front and program building, and organization and stragic building and planning with progressive and revolutionary forces in tin America Latin America, the Caribbean and throughout the African Diaspora and with the world anti-imperialist, anti-Zionist movements and struggles and genuine socialist building governments and organizations and positive forces. It is within the major organization work and tasks of this phase that the initial and ongoing contacts and relationships are made for the building of an international coordinate struggle. One clear example of this was the international travels that Malcolm X was making during the latter part of his life {1963 to 1965} and the contacts that his organizational efforts were making with African revolutionary leaders in African and the building of a relationship with revolutionary China and Cuba. We can also look at the domestic and international activities of the Black Panther Party, the Black Panther Party for Self-Defense. the Revolutionary Action Movement and the All African People's Revolutionary Party and of course the national liberation struggles and movements of Africa, Latin America, the Caribbean and Asia. To contemplate the building of community power in the US, organizational development and a revolutionary struggle in isolation of the world struggle – and for African people particularly, the world-wide Africa struggle, would be more than myopic, it would be disastrous and downright stupid! With such understanding and review of the strategies, and mistakes of the organizations and struggles just mentioned are many lessons and models for building a movement, organization building and networking and meaningful and mass empowering community development and without doubt for the making of people's revolution.

During this phase {pre-revolutionary crisis period, and within the context of progressive reformist and especially revolutionary organizations, there must be emphasis on careful buildup of political, social, and economic organizations. Mass consciousness, vanguard and mass organization building work, community influence, institution building, community control and self-reliance are major concerns during this phase. <u>The accomplishments of this current phase within the US is crucial for the next phase, the revolutionary crisis.</u>

In this phase because of **objective and subjective conditions** a change has taken place in the power and control situations in a country. The oppressor power - as a result of the systemic contradictions of **capitalism** - is in a situation of crisis and desperation. Because of the oppressive conditions and the growing resistance to oppression the government does not have the strong hold on society as it did in an enemy held situation. **In terms of objective conditions**, there is much instability within the economic structure, financial institutions and the country is characterized by political-economic instability. For example, America today is rapidly approaching this situation, in spite of the fact that there is yet much disorganization and lack of consciousness among the oppressed, particularly the African and Latino oppressed.

Many of the **objective conditions** for revolution exist in America. This is characterized by the intense oppression of the people, high unemployment, drastic health conditions, poor housing, repression on political organizations, rising prison populations, poor education, economic crisis, massive downsizing, rising discontent and resentment towards the government, intensification of class struggle among the oppress, increased racism, increased gender oppression, increased corruption within the government, disunity among the oppressive ruling class, division within the armies of the ruling classes, defeat in military operations of the government, mayhem of capitalist production, intense competitive price wars being waged among all the major sectors of the American corporate industry, massive layoffs, less investment and fierce competition among investors, comprehensive business failures and bankruptcies, fewer jobs, less consumption and even less reason for business to invest, increased and intense criminalization of the youth, student dissent on a massive –national scale, massive anti-war protest and demonstrations, social misery and health conditions become epidemic, rise in radicalism and people resistance, comprehensive distrust of government, massive and nationally destabilizing protests and demonstrations, lack of confidence in government and elected officials, system destabilize strikes, consumer alarm and growing panic, rise in crime rate- poverty breeds crime, rise in inflation and impending depression, increase trade deficit and trade wars, government and economic policy based on desperation, the rise of a police state and fascism, the reliance on repression and police terror replacing the ability to control and mislead by way of distraction(*media-brainwashing, sports and entertainment distraction, drugs and mis-education, family destabilization and strategies to encourage and induce fear.*) The oppressor relies more and more on brute force to maintain control. In this situation, it becomes clearer every day that the government and economy is crumbling and unable to meet even basis needs of the people! These objective conditions mentioned are the things that revolutionary crises is made of. As you are aware many of these conditions already exist in America in 2011. It will only get geometrically worse in 2012 and on towards the fall of the American government and collapse of its' political-economic system!

The length of each phase depends on the changes between the enemy forces and peoples, and also on the changes in the international situation and its relation to positive organizational forces within the people's struggle. ***This is why the demand of mass consciousness and organization along with building international relations and alliances are crucial in this and all phases.***

Currently the necessary primary subjective conditions within the struggle of the masses do not yet exist amongst the people. In the U.S. - among Africans and Latinos masses for example - the subjective

122

conditions of wide spread cultural, nationalistic, anti-government and revolutionary consciousness is very weak and for the most part does not exist in any mass-organized manner. Yet, oppression can breed resistance ad consciousness. **This reality indicates some of the immediate tasks of this period.** In specific terms, the subjective conditions must be the programmatic actions of revolutionaries – *particularly in the pre-revolutionary and revolutionary crisis phases* – by this we mean: mass consciousness, working unity between organizations, community institution building, effective and politically consolidated coalitions and united fronts, significant numbers of the people in organization - particularly revolutionary organizations, the initial and further development of mass revolutionary political parties and "preparation and development" of the people's revolutionary armies. Although these vital subjective factors do not currently exist within the context of the struggle with the US – **to the degree that they must be built** - history does give proof that such factors do and will develop! *The objectives conditions help provide the needed subjective factors, and the development of the subjective factors take advantage of the objective conditions.* The successful accomplishments of the tasks of this phase are the material conditions that provide for making an enemy held zone become a contested zone. Consequently, some of the requirement during the pre-revolutionary crisis phases are:

- ☐ Identification and development of a conscious core of revolutionaries and cadre development and strategic placement within the mass experience and struggle.

- ☐ Development of a conscious core and placement of the conscious core with the sectors of the people when and where mass resistance and struggle is at its highest point of positive action.(add footnote)

- ☐ Institution building in terms of organization and neighborhood/community power bases Programmatic interaction and networking among African organizations- leading up to building of an African united front.

- [ ] Development of Revolutionary Pan-African relationships and alliances with world revolutionary, socialist, anti-imperialist and progressive forces.

- [ ] Mass positive action

- [ ] Building of militant independent party and an all-African Revolutionary Pan-African political party

  Within these seven areas are the basis for the alternative to US neo-liberal policies and its current and very deceptive {Black Ace card - the feeble and essentially weak "puppet put on show" of the Obama-drama}

- [ ] Identification and development of a conscious core of revolutionaries, cadre development and strategic placement within the mass experience and struggle.

Practice without thought is empty; thought without practice is blind. History is the movement of the dialectic – the continuous movement of positive and negative forces; and of course, the hand of GOD is omnipresence and always behind the scene. *We act the way we think, and for conscious action, there must be a social-political basis of thought guiding it partly arising from the mass of reality and in tune affecting it.* It can be convincingly argued that matter is primary, but ideas are critical to guide the direction in which matter will develop. The need for a conscious, highly skilled force of organizers is a vital perquisite for social alterations, social reform, social movements and revolution. This conscious core must be guided by correct ideology and strategy and dedicated to the purpose. Then their strategic placement and/or involvement in the segment of the people where the dialectic for forward movement and change is most dynamic are required. This core of the conscious can serve as a catalyst, spark and mass inspired vanguard force; it cannot be a vanguard in any elitist or Marxist sense; in other words, this writer highlights a rejection of the view that the people cannot make their own history. The internal dynamic is the basis for change!

Thousands of cadre cells or circles must be developed. They must be organized throughout the people in as many sectors of the people as possible. This is a tactical issue of identifying the pulse of the people's response to oppression and their pro-active struggle for betterment and assessing the degree, and form of engaging struggle, using the situation to ameliorate a problem while at the same time advancing the dialectic forward- organizing around the peoples attempts and aspirations to rid themselves of oppression and exploitation while building the revolutionary struggle towards more organize and mass endeavors. This is a matter of mass development or strategic involvement within the mass and organizing. These nuclei of conscious organizers must be made to exist throughout the organism of the mass of the people. Even though the core organizers may not be able to immediately implement much of the revolutionary theory they are learning, they must study ad discuss it nevertheless and engage in the struggle for development as part of the mass. Consequently, revolutionaries must find themselves involved in reformist work to advance it towards revolution!

"Dialectics inform us that when the negative dominates, the positive is reform it becomes an obsolete on the road to freedom; it must give way to revolution."

The reforms mention in the book will not avoid revolution; rather, rather they will help advance the African revolution and consequently the world socialist revolution." {See: Black Power, The Politics of Liberation: Stokely Carmichael and Charles Hamilton}

☐ **Institution building in terms of organization and neighborhood/community Power bases.**

☐ **"Integration was a subterfuge for the maintenance of White power. Africans in the Democratic party represent powerlessness visibility."** *{See: Black Power, The Politics of Liberation: Stokely Carmichael and Charles Hamilton}*

The quote above implies that ultimately, oppress people can only look to GOD and themselves regarding the ending of their oppression. Most certainly the cannot look to their oppressor nor their oppressors' solutions. One of the essential aspirations and demands of the genuine Black Power, Africa nationalist and developing revolutionary Pan-African movement of the sixties was the reverberating insistence for cultural integrity and self-sufficiency; *the right of African people to be independent of western and colonial thought, to define our own reality, our own intentions and our own destiny!* This enlighten path towards development stands unconditionally in opposition to integration or any assimilationist policy. It is not about trying to prove ourselves to America nor is it about trying to be all that America expects but to focus - primarily – on our cultural development and power to insure that we are in continuous control of our development - a development that is not in the interest of American capitalism. A prerequisite for this is institution building in terms of organization and neighborhood/community power bases.

THE SEARCH FOR NEW FORMS

It is imperative to build bases of power in the community by way of organizational cooperation and collective efforts and by doing, so turn our community into a base of power. We must strive to at least have much more political influence moving towards control of our schools in our communities, the hospitals, stores, spiritual centers, colonial agencies and executive, judicial and legislative arms of the colonial machine. We must strive to at least have much more political influence moving towards control of the executive, legislative and judicial arms of the colonial machine and make it move in our interest or make it weak, dysfunctional or non-effective. We must have control of the colony or make it uncontrollable by the enemy.

☐ **Development of Revolutionary Pan-African relationships and alliances with world revolutionary, socialist, anti-imperialist and progressive forces.**

Around the world, African people are over two billion strong. While it is utterly romantic to think that all African people can be united into a force for liberation and good, it is quite feasible and in fact essential that a quality mass force { including millions of people } can be developed in the interest of Africa people. We must build an international and coordinated force for Africa and African people's development and cultural self-sufficiency. Political relationships with revolutionary Africa and with African revolutionary forces of African people in the Diaspora must be built. Alliance with the progressive forces of the world must be built. Relationships of cooperation and strategic planning must be built with the socialist and anti-imperialist forces of the world. An isolationist strategy has no place in the liberation efforts of African people. Every community organization needs to have an agenda that includes aspects of this need for relationship building. TO MAKE THIS EFFECTIVE THE AFRICAN MUST BE WITHIN STRONG ORGANIZATION!

☐ **Programmatic interaction and networking among African organizations- leading up to building of an African united front.**

Positive action must overwhelm negative action and this must manifest in mass involvement in organization, mass consciousness rising, and significant increase in the interaction and programmatic relationships among African organizations. Unity must not just be a slogan but a reality. Africans must be in organization and African organizations must be about a coordinated strategy leading toward very broad organizational coalitions, formations for development and liberation and genuine African united fronts and Revolutionary Pan-African coordination and organization. Such a strategy should even envision the organizational relationship with the indigenous and Latino forces of positive action.

With regards to African people, this must take place wherever African people are. My experience and research has informed me that this fact must be emphasized on the continent and in the Diaspora but it is particularly in the Diaspora area of the US that this point must be emphasized the most. Particularly because of this point I have added this Special Note to Africans in America and also because it appears that nowhere is the Obama deception more prevalent than in the US, among Africans who have been the victims of racist-capitalist Americanism!

Special Note to African in America

Careful analysis of this strategy and how it relates to the Revolutionary Pan-African movement and the vanguard position of the African in the developing revolutionary struggle in the Diaspora, particularly the struggle of Africans, and other people of color, especially the most populous in the Western hemisphere who exist in a varieties of sectors and are commonly referred to as Latino or Indian people. Each zone in the Diaspora has a crucial role to play in an international strategy to defeat imperialism. The African and the oppressed people of color in the western hemisphere have a crucial role in the Revolutionary Pan-African movement and the defeat of US led world imperialism. In coordination with the struggle in Africa, a combined African –Latino strategy can bring about a decisive blow to the US and is essential to the

128

destabilization, defeat and overthrow of the US government. The US has long tried to prevent such an alliance and is well aware of its revolutionary potential in nit only the US but throughout Latin America. A closer analysis of this potential leads to a strategy for revolutionary victory in Latin America and the US.

No one knows capitalism like the African! We know it from the rape, exploitation and penetration of Mother Africa up to the current oppression and exploitation of the African neighborhoods and communities of the Africa world of today. The African has unfortunately been an integral part of American capitalism. We have labored and died to build it. In fact, it has been built on the backs of the African. As soon as we **GET UP AND STAND UP FOR OUR RIGHTS AND DIGITY**, capitalism will come tumbling down. As soon as the African in America, throughout the Diaspora and in Africa start acting in a truly self-reliant and independent manner the American capitalist system and government is disaster-prone!

The resistance of Africans to capitalism has never totally abated and will not stop until we organize and fight our way to our total and just liberation. African people are moving towards freedom and no power on earth can stop us. In spite of the devastation of capitalism, the Revolutionary Pan-African movement marches forward.

As a result of the racist-capitalist slave commerce, African people are scattered and suffering in many parts of the world. Revolutionary Pan-Africanism is correct, the core of the Black revolution is in Africa, and until Africa is free the, the black man (woman) lacks a national home: Africans of the world must be cognizant of our political responsibilities, no matter where we are in the world!

All Africans - no matter where they are in the world - have a responsibility to join or create organization wherever they are. By way of people's mass organization and revolutionary parties, the struggles of Africans in all parts of the world must recognize the necessity to control

129

the African community, zone or African country where they reside in , while at the same time helping to build a coordinated struggle - **worldwide** - between Africa communities and countries with Africa as the core. ***Of course, even this is relative and interdependent with the advances and successes of the African Revolution of African soil!*** Consequently the - worldwide - African revolutionary struggle can be divided into zones or hemispheres of struggle. North America, for example, must be seen as a zone of the African Revolution - *as a matter of strategy, moral principle and historical truth*! It cannot be viewed as a liberation struggle that is separate and not an integral part of the African Revolution. Africans in America cannot view themselves as a different or "new" type of African. Yes, our experiences in America in a sense, is new and in that sense, unique, but the struggles of Africans in other parts of the Diaspora is also "new" and unique. That does not make Africans in one part of the Diaspora a different people. The advances of the liberation struggle in one area is really meaningless without the liberation of Africans as a whole. No African is free unless the masses of Africans everywhere are free, and again, the core of any Africa struggle has been and will always take shape around the continent of Africa. The African revolution must be seen as one struggle with a variety of unique situations based on geography and historical experiences, for sure, but basically, the struggle of African people has an overall unity of history and oppression. Our response to that oppression has always been basically in common. The African revolution is one, with **one goal, one aim and one destiny!**

Such a strategic view demands responsibilities for Africans in each strategic zone. With respect to North America, there is a tremendous amount of work to be done. For sure, Africans in America are the most technologically advanced mass of Africans in the world. We Africans in America live in one of the most crucial and strategic nerve centers of US led imperialism. (Of course not losing sight of the fact that the "**most crucial nerve center for imperialism**" is the neo-colonial hold on Africa). Africans in America have more exposure to resources, technical

130

equipment and information than Africans in any other part of the world; they are captives behind enemy lines with enormous potential to give support to the Mother land and to neutralize, disrupt, destabilize and destroy vital political, economic and military capitalist infrastructure, yet, considering all this potential and accessibility, the African in America is one of the most politically backward, unorganized and unconscious Africans than anywhere in the world. This is pathetically horrendous and culturally irresponsible. I hate to say this about us Africans in North America, but it is true. Such a "hard line" and bitter assessment is not new ; it was said over forty years ago by a person that no responsible African would dare to challenge, Big Red!

The Revolutionary Pan-Africanist Malcolm X was just as critical about Africans in America. His acid criticism was contained in his immortal speech, "Message To The Grass Roots," where he gave a class analysis in speaking of the house Negro and the field Negro.

A closer look at the strategy of U.S. imperialism to prevent capitalist destabilization and a seizure of power inside of the US and Latin America shows how fundamental a coordinated assault by way of the defeat of neo-colonialism in Africa can set the US up for a frontal attack within the confines of the US. Also, the positive reaction on the part of the revolutionary movement of Africans and Latino in America and throughout the Western hemisphere reveals the power and potential anti-capitalist threat of a combined African-Latino-Western indigenous resiliency for revolutionary production and is a pointer to the inevitable conquest of good over evil and positive action over negative reaction within the geo-political context of the United snakes! This must not be underestimated by those who seek the overthrown of the American capitalist system and the corrupt government and armed forces that seek to maintain its existence.

131

☐ **The building of a militant independent party and/or an all-African Revolutionary Pan-African political party is essential**

"OUR VICTORY IS INEVITABLE FOR GOD IS ON OUR SIDE. THE ONLY QUESTION IS WHAT ROLW WILL YOU, WILL YOR ORGANIZATION PLAY IN THIS INEVITABLE REALITY."

Minister Gideon Odinga Mukhtar
I APPRCIATE YOUR COMMENTS
tiger_osinga@yajhoo.com

About the Author

Odinga Mukhtar is a Revolutionary Pan-African, minister, author, professor and father and grandfather. He has had over thirty-five years of struggling experience in the Civil Rights, Black power and Revolutionary Pan-African Movement. He has, by way of  organizations he has been a part of, worked with a number of African leaders including Seoul Toure, Kwame Ture, Bob Brown, Assata Shakur, Almicar Cabral, Thomas Sankara, Bob Marley and many others.

He has helped continue the Pan-Africanists legacy at home and abroad. His numerous articles and writings champions the cause and contribution of Africa's greatest daughters like M'balia Camara, Anna Julia Cooper, Shirley Graham Dubois, Amy Ashwood and Amy Jacques Garvey, Queen Mother Moore, and countless other mothers and sisters of Africa who served, sacrificed and suffered so that Africa and Africans may be liberated and united. He is a professor for the Pan-African Studies Continuing Education Program at Temple University and a columnist for the Black Star Community newspaper in Philadelphia, PA; and a minister of Yeshua Temple of Praise. Minister Odinga now resides in Savannah, GA.